Fighting the Good Fight

Healing and Advocacy after Clergy Sexual Assault

by Carolyn Waterstradt, MA, MSW

Fighting the Good Fight

Healing and Advocacy after Clergy Sexual Assault

Cover design by Jacob Kubon.

Published by

splatteredinkpress.com

ISBN 978-0-9848542-7-1

The Phoenix hope, can wing her way through the desert skies,
and still defying fortune's spite;
revive from ashes and rise.

—Miguel de Cervantes

This book is dedicated to all who have been wounded by clergy sexual assault.

There is hope for a wonderful, new life!

—C.W.

embedded in society—that clergypersons are holier than others and would never "do such a thing." These stories of blame create a sense of shame, guilt, and responsibility in women concerning the abusive relationship. In this book, I attempt to shift this paradigm by assigning new language to victimization.

Virgin and Laborer

The terms "victim," "survivor," and "thriver" are usually used to describe the healing process a woman undergoes after she has been sexually assaulted. However, these terms create the illusion that healing is linear and make it difficult for women to move beyond the victim stage. This is especially true if victims are continuously being revictimized by the members of their congregation, leaders in their denomination, or others. It is difficult for them to heal when others are gossiping and telling damaging stories about them, accusing them of being at fault, or trying to silence them about the matter. To shift the victim paradigm of blame and shame, I have chosen to use the term "virgin" to refer to women who are being groomed for sexual assault or are being sexually assaulted by a member of the clergy.

"Virgin" was chosen because the eighteen women I interviewed for this book, regardless of their past sexual experiences, were all virgins in their faith prior to clergy sexual assault. Just as people who are virgins physically are naïve about sex, spiritual virgins are naïve about the clergy and spirituality. As virgins, they trust a representative of God to act in a morally upright manner, just as the church has conditioned them to believe he will. They come seeking counsel, guidance, mentoring, spiritual direction, or supervision from a representative of God who uses a position of trust to be abusive. In most, if not all, cases, after the experience of clergy sexual assault shatters a virgin's spiritual innocence, she is left struggling to recreate her life, her identity, her faith, and her spirituality. Her spiritual innocence is gone.

After virgins are free of the abusive relationship, they become what I call "laborers." Healing from clergy sexual assault is much like the birth process as the laborer gives birth to a new creation. Granted, we must be a bit flexible with this analogy because in this context the laborer and the newborn are one and the same human being; still, I believe the image works. There are many contractions and labor pains to breathe through as a laborer is birthed into a new creation. Some labors are longer and more difficult than others. Some labors stop progressing after they have started. Some end in disappointment, some in tragedy. But just as advances in modern medicine have reduced the number of deaths during the birthing process, so, too, can a laboring plan after clergy sexual assault aid laborers in their rebirth. This book attempts to be the beginnings of such a plan.

A woman who has given birth does not return to being the exact same woman she was prior to giving birth. She has been altered by the pregnancy and birth process. Her hips have widened, stretch marks remain, the stomach is no longer toned, and she has become more acutely aware of the need to create a safe world for all children.

Just as the mother is altered by the birth process, so, too, are laborers healing from clergy sexual assault altered. Their identity, their spirituality, virtually their entire lives will need to be rebirthed in light of the assault. The stretch marks across the birth-mother's abdomen never fade completely, and neither does the memory of labor following clergy sexual assault. So, many laborers become aware of the need to create a safety net for other vulnerable virgins. After a laborer has experienced some form of rebirth, she may choose to become a spiritual "midwife." Midwives labor with those in pain by allowing the wisdom of their own experience to permeate a hurting, broken world.

When viewed in terms of labor, the aftermath of clergy sexual assault becomes an expectant opportunity. Labor pains are transformed into discoveries of dark and beautiful truths about oneself and the Sacred. The time a laborer spends in spiritual isolation and desolation can take her breath away just as painful contractions take the breath away from the laboring mother. But as the laborer learns to breathe and relax through these contractions, the darkness becomes a pregnant possibility where opportunities of rebirth occur.

Although the terms "virgin" and "laborer" are used throughout this book, at times I have chosen to use the terms "victim" and "survivor" in order not to superimpose my terminology on someone else's research, writing, or interview.

Religion

Spirituality and religion are often intertwined, and their definitions are broad. In this book, James Fowler's definition of "religion" will be used. Fowler defines religion as the vehicle linking human beings "to communities of shared memory and shared hope." These communities symbolize the human condition and allow visions to be enacted that can animate and give new life.[1] Many laborers are forced from their religious com-

---

1 James W. Fowler, *Stages of Faith: The Psychology of Human Development and the Quest for Meaning* (San Francisco: Harper, 1981), 294.

munity, and finding new community is difficult for them. Part of healing is coming to terms with the role community will play in their lives.

Spirituality

I use Rita Nakashima Brock's feminist definition of "spirituality." Brock describes spirituality as connectedness, and feminist spirituality as "both radically political and deeply personal, uniting the struggle of women to free themselves from male dominance and the need for personal, bodily integrity."[2] Brock contends that Western society is based on patriarchal religious concepts such as "masculine deities, a male clerical class, and ideologies of female subordination, including women's physical weakness and uncleanness, and emotional and moral inferiority."[3] In addition, Brock contends that patriarchy is evident in Christianity because, despite the fact that in the U.S. one-third of women have been raped, one-fourth of girls and one-eighth of boys have been molested, and "every thirty-nine seconds a woman is battered in her own home,"[4] churches remain virtually silent on these issues.

Women in the midst of healing from clergy sexual assault are thrown into the struggle of freeing themselves to some extent from patriarchal religious constructs and systems. Even women who were sexually assaulted by a member of the clergy and remain within organized religious structures undergo a process of feminizing their beliefs and solidifying their

---

[2] Rita Nakashima Brock, *Journey by Heart: A Christology of Erotic Power* (New York: Crossroad, 1988), 22.
[3] Ibid, 5.
[4] Ibid, 3.

integrity. This is accomplished as they come to trust themselves as the authority of what they believe.

Naming

Because many of the laborers had difficulty naming God after their assaults, sometimes terms such as "Higher Power," "Mystery," and "Spirit" are used. In keeping with the Jewish tradition, when the Jewish laborer speaks, the Divine Name is written as "G-d."

All abusive clergy in this book have been given the pseudonym Joe.

Section Preview

This book is divided into five sections. Section I defines the problem of clergy sexual assault and describes its history in the United States.

Section II is the result of research interviews I conducted individually with eighteen laborers regarding their healing process. Chapter 3 provides a theological and spiritual foundation for healing after clergy sexual assault, while chapters 4 through 6 share what was learned through the interviews. In chapter 7, I share my own story of healing after clergy sexual assault, and also address why and how the process of researching and writing the book was transformative for me.

Section III contains the voices of others interviewed whose lives have been touched by clergy sexual assault: two husbands of laborers, the mother of a laborer, a minister who worked with a woman after her victimization, and a chaplain who belonged to a congregation whose pastor assaulted many of his congregants.

Section IV includes recommendations for an entire community that has been impacted by clergy sexual assault. This section contains specific chapters for laborers, family and friends, religious organizations, mental health professionals, legislators and policy advocates, and researchers. Each chapter contains brief guidelines such as how to work through the assault, how to put safeguards in place to protect virgins and laborers, and areas in need of further exploration.

I chose to use the pronoun "you" in some chapters, especially 14 and 15, which specifically address people who are struggling directly with clergy sexual assault; using the second-person pronoun seemed much more supportive and personal than writing in the third person.

The fifth section offers appendices, as well as other resources the reader may find helpful, such as a Recommended Reading list and a glossary. I have used an appendix format to offer those who are interested the theories, limitations, and methodologies of my research.

Although the book reads best in sequence, as most chapters build on information contained in previous chapters, each chapter can be read individually. Those in Section IV were particularly designed to be shared by the laborer with others in her support network. For example, a laborer may read this book and desire to share chapter 15 with family and chapter 17 with her therapist. However, in order to understand the terminology in these chapters, readers may find it helpful to read the first part of this introduction or use the glossary.

Although many individual chapters of this book could be expanded into books of their own, the chapters are designed to give an overview in order to bring understanding and, hopefully, healing to people whose lives have been affected by clergy sexual assault. In writing *Fighting the Good Fight*, my intention was, and is, that it be a healing guide and educational tool to the reader, and that it give struggling laborers hope that life can be fulfilling and meaningful after clergy sexual assault.

SECTION I

The Problem

If a gem falls into mud, it will still remain valuable.

—Saadi of Shiraz

Chapter 1

What Is Clergy Assault?

People rarely think of a clergyperson's sexual relationship with an adult congregant as abusive. Rather, such relationships are often viewed as consensual and the woman is frequently blamed or portrayed as the seductress, as in the novel *The Thorn Birds.*[5] Yet this portrayal is absolutely incorrect. Such relationships are *always* abusive due to the power a clergyperson holds as a result of his[6] position.

Because most congregants believe clergy are called by God to the ministry and are God's representatives, congregants tend to automatically trust their clergyperson to be morally upright. Congregants seldom afford such blanket trust to people who are not clergy. For this reason, no matter how consensual the virgin believes her sexual relationship to be with her clergy person, it is *never* consensual, even if it appears so. The amount of spiritual and psychological coercion involved in these relationships, the power that the clergy holds, and the soul wound inflicted on the virgin make it impossible for such a relationship to be consensual.

Perhaps this makes more sense if we think first about how we react to and what we call one-time or ongoing sexual relations between a clergyperson (or any adult, for that matter)

---

[5] Colleen McCullough, *The Thorn Birds,* (New York: Avon Books, 1977).

[6] Although female clergy can abuse members of their congregation, clergy sexual assault is predominantly perpetrated by male clergy. For this reason the male pronoun will be used for clergy.

and a child. Clearly, we are incensed at such occurrences! We name them what they are: *sexual abuse*. In no way do we blame the child, even if he or she is an older teen, because many in our society have come to understand that there is a power differential between such a young person and the adult who makes improper sexual advances against him or her.

Such is also precisely the case when a member of the clergy draws into a sexual relationship an adult woman (or, conceivably, a man) who is his congregant, counselee, occupational subordinate, or simply someone who looks up to him as a clergyperson.

Let's look at some basic, and fairly standard, definitions of terms I use in this book.

Clergy Sexual Assault

Sometimes the phrase "clergy sexual misconduct" is used to refer to the sexual exploitation of an adult by a member of the clergy. However "'misconduct' does not capture the exploitation, betrayal of trust, and destruction" a clergyperson's behavior causes when he sexually exploits a congregant.[7] The phrase "clergy sexual abuse" is also used to refer to this sexual exploitation, but to many people it implies that the abused was a child. Because both terms can be misleading and because clergy sexual misconduct is legally defined by some states, such as Arkansas and Texas, as criminal sexual assault, the term "clergy sexual assault" is used throughout this book to refer to clergy engaging in sexual relationships with congregants, counselees, or co-workers. However, at times, the

---

[7] Diana R. Garland, "When Wolves Wear Shepherds' Clothing," *Social Work and Christianity* 33, no. 1 (2006), 1–35.

terms "misconduct" and "abuse" are used so as not to superimpose this terminology on others.

Grooming

Before a clergyperson sexually assaults a congregant, a period of grooming often takes place. The grooming period involves the clergyperson choosing a virgin and then working closely with her to gradually wear down her boundaries. The clergyperson anticipates that the end result of the relationship will be sexual in nature. Grooming usually happens by means of boundary violations that start small and grow larger as the clergyperson subtly breaks down a virgin's defenses and confuses her.

Such grooming might include the following:

- Inviting a virgin to do special things outside the church setting, such as attending a seminar together in which they both share an interest. This is especially likely to be grooming behavior if other signs of grooming are present.
- Sharing confidential information about other congregants.
- Brushing up inappropriately against a virgin, often in such a way that the virgin believes it was accidental, as a means of breaking down a virgin's physical boundaries.
- Scheduling counseling sessions or meetings when no one is in the church building, or scheduling sessions at the virgin's home or the clergyperson's home when no one else is there.

- Touching a virgin during a counseling session—for example, putting his arm around her while she cries, kissing her forehead in a fatherly manner, or kissing her cheek and telling her it was the kiss of peace. Though often perceived by the woman as fatherly or brotherly concern, such gestures are never appropriate and tend to confuse the virgin.
- Expressing love for the virgin, usually first in the context of brotherly, Christian, agape, courtly, or spiritual love.
- Saying things like "No one has ever understood me like you do" or "God sent you to me."
- Making an obscene gesture or remark.
- Reversing roles—for example, telling the virgin that she is helping him in some manner, such as healing him spiritually or psychologically. It is inappropriate for this healing responsibility to be placed on a virgin, just as it is inappropriate for a therapist to expect such from a client, or a teacher to expect such from a student.
- Revealing intimate details of his life to the virgin when they are alone, which is another form of role reversal. If he has a need to share intimately, licensed therapists and his family and friends can fulfill this need.
- Sharing dissatisfaction about his wife with the virgin.
- Asking for details regarding a virgin's marriage, especially if the virgin is not seeing him for marriage counseling.
- Asking for information about the virgin's sex life. Most clergy are not trained as sex therapists.
- Giving a virgin material that is sexual in nature.
- Using Scripture, tradition, liturgy, or terms like "spiritual twin" or "spiritual partner" to justify a physical or love relationship.

- Using the virgin's spiritual, emotional, or psychological vulnerabilities to manipulate her. This might be difficult to detect until after the relationship has ended.

Frequency and Factors

Clergy sexual assault of adult women happens with some regularity in religious organizations. A study whose results were published in 2009 found that 3.1 percent of "women who attend religious services at least monthly reported being the object of a sexual advance by a clergyperson or religious leader since turning 18,"[8] though the study fails to account for the number of women who were assaulted and no longer attend religious services. The United Church of Canada's denominational report on sexual abuse found that "women are more likely to get sexually harassed in the church than in the workplace and that clergy were sexually exploiting their parishioners at twice the rate of secular therapists."[9] A 2003 study of male and female Lutheran clergy found that 10.5 percent reported committing sexual misconduct, but it was hypothesized that if only male clergy had been surveyed, the percentage would likely have been higher because female clergy tend not to commit sexual misconduct as frequently as male clergy.[10] A survey of three hundred ministers in the

[8] Mark Chaves and Diana R. Garland, "The Prevalence of Clergy Sexual Advances Toward Adults in Their Congregations," *Journal for the Scientific Study of Religion* 48 (2009), 817–824.
[9] Stanley J. Gernz and Roy D. Bell, *Betrayal of Trust* (Grand Rapids: Baker Books, 1995), 24.
[10] Perry C. Francis and James Stacks, "The Association between Spiritual Well-Being and Clergy Sexual Misconduct," *Journal of Religion and Abuse* 5 (2003), 79–100.

United States found that "39 percent reported sexual contact and 12.7 percent actual sexual intercourse with a congregant. In addition, 76.5 percent indicated that they knew of a minister who they believed had engaged in sexual intercourse with a congregant."[11] A study of Church of England clergy found that 67 percent knew of a peer who had been sexually involved with a member of his congregation.[12] According to a study done by the Center for the Prevention of Sexual and Domestic Violence in Seattle, 70 percent of Southern Baptist ministers knew of a minister who had committed sexual misconduct with a congregant.[13] It should also be noted that many of these are likely not reports of isolated incidents as Rev. Dr. Marie Fortune illustrates in *Is Nothing Sacred?*[14] My research also indicates that in many cases abusive clergy groom and assault multiple victims.

After interviewing sixty-one primary and secondary victims, social scientists Diane R. Garland and Christen Argueta identified five factors that contribute to clergy sexual misconduct.[15] First, they identified that victims were unable to recognize they were being groomed for a sexual relationship by their clergyperson because they trusted him as the moral authority of the church. Their trust in him caused them to doubt their

---

[11] Stanley J. Gernz and Roy D. Bell, *Betrayal of Trust*, 24.
[12] Thaddeus Birchard, "Clergy Sexual Misconduct: Frequency and Causation," *Sexual and Relationship Therapy* 15 (2000), 127–139.
[13] Gayle White, "Sexual Misconduct: Keeping Vigil: How Various Faiths Protect the Innocent in Their Flocks," *Atlanta Journal-Constitution* (September 14, 2002), B1.
[14] Marie Fortune, *Is Nothing Sacred?: The Story of a Pastor, the Women He Sexually Abused, and the Congregation He Nearly Destroyed* (Cleveland: United Church Press, 1999).
[15] Diana R. Garland and Christen Argueta, "How Clergy Sexual Misconduct Happens: A Qualitative Study of First-Hand Accounts," *Social Work and Christianity* 37 (2010): 1-35.

ability to discern the inappropriateness of his actions, although many victims stated that they would have interpreted the same behaviors as inappropriate had they been done by any other man. For example, one victim, after her priest had been sexually inappropriate with her, said, "I convinced myself that it was just a mistake after all, that my imagination was running wild, and that a priest wouldn't attempt something sexual with me or anyone."[16] This inability of victims to trust their instincts also extends to victims' family members and to other congregants. After one man's wife came home from a retreat and told him she had been skinny-dipping with the pastor, the study quotes him as saying, "I wanted to say, 'What are you doing?' I wanted to call my parents. But then it got smoothed over, and the worry went away."[17]

The confusion of blending sexual advances with spirituality often causes victims to mistrust their perceptions and dismiss the grooming behavior, sometimes blaming themselves for the clergyperson's sexual advances.

The second contributing factor Garland and Argueta identified is the culture of niceness in the United States that excuses people's inappropriate behavior. We do not want to offend, hurt, or embarrass others, so we tend to downplay or dismiss inappropriate behavior.

Third, many clergy have a lack of accountability. Often they are the only full-time staff-person in the congregation, which enables them to spend much of their time counseling whomever they want, whenever they want, wherever they want.

Fourth, the clergyperson serves multiple and overlapping roles with his victims. For example, many clergy not only

---

[16] Ibid, 10.
[17] Ibid, 12.

act as God's representative, but also fill such roles as therapist, spiritual director, friend, confidante, or parental figure to their congregants. Except under rare conditions, it is unethical for therapists to hold multiple or overlapping relationships with their clients as such relationships can be damaging. However, clergy do not have this ethical standard and do hold overlapping and multiple relationships with their congregants, often seeing them outside of church activities. This can give clergy tremendous power over congregants and creates greater opportunities for them to violate professional boundaries.

Fifth, the victims in Garland and Argueta's study believed the church was a sanctuary where congregants could be vulnerable without fear of being manipulated or exploited. In fact, it had never occurred to them that clergy could act in an abusive, exploitative manner.

Soul Wound

The clergyperson's manipulation causes some virgins to feel they are being brainwashed by their religious leader or trapped in the toxic relationship. Feeling cornered, they tend to remain silent. Once they do tell or the relationship is discovered, they are often revictimized by the collusion or lack of response of other clergy and church leaders, and shamed and blamed by members of their congregation. As a result of the assault, laborers are frequently forced out of their congregations. Some lose friends and family members. Others lose careers because they either were employed by the congregation or are too traumatized by the sexual assault to hold a job.

In times of need, many people turn to religion or spirituality to sustain them. However, most laborers are unable to find such comfort because their spiritual beliefs have been compromised by the combination of sexual exploitation with religion and spirituality. It becomes difficult for the laborer to separate God from the offending clergyperson, the assault, and the church as a whole, and this hinders her faith. Clergy betrayal also makes it hard for laborers to trust others, the church, and God because they often wonder, if they cannot trust those who represent God, whom *can* they trust?

As a result of losing so much, laborers undergo intense grieving and experience many symptoms of sexual assault (see the boxes on page 21).[18] Some are hospitalized with severe depression or suicidal ideation. Some develop the psychological condition known as post-traumatic stress disorder (PTSD). People suffering from PTSD often see the world as unsafe and unpredictable, which tends to create an existential predicament and alter their religious and spiritual beliefs.[19]

To determine how the religious beliefs and attitudes had changed in women who experienced severe adversity, Marleen Williams, a social scientist at Brigham Young University, and three of her colleagues studied Jewish, Christian, and Muslim women who had experienced such adversity.[20] Some of the traumatic events experienced by the women studied were

---

[18] Candace R. Benyei, *Understanding Clergy Misconduct in Religious Systems* (New York: Haworth Pastoral Press, 1998), 173-174. Some information in the box is also based on my own work with laborers.
[19] Jonathan R. T. Davidson, Kathryn M. Connor, and Li-Ching Lee, "Beliefs in Karma and Reincarnation among Survivors of Violent Trauma: A Community Survey," *Social Psychiatry and Psychiatric Epidemiology* 40 (2005) 120-125; Sherry A. Falsetti, Patricia A. Resick, and Joanne L. Davis, "Changes in Religious Beliefs Following Trauma," *Journal of Traumatic Stress* 16 (2003) 391-398.
[20] Marleen S. Williams, Annette Jerome, Kirsten White, and Aaron Fisher, "Making Sense of Suffering: A Preliminary Study of Changes in Religious Women Adjusting to Severe Adversity," *Counseling and Values* 50 (2006): 84-98.

illness resulting in the amputation of both legs and all fingers, a husband developing Huntington's chorea, and one of the women falling asleep at the wheel, causing death or grave injury to family members and herself. The study found that all the women's religious beliefs and attitudes had changed, though differences did present depending on the faith tradition to which they belonged.

Although PTSD typically contains spiritual and existential elements, because laborers' trauma happened in a religious setting, their spiritual and existential struggle often becomes a prominent symptom of their assault and PTSD. This is especially true if they have been alienated from their religious community. Laborers' very *souls* are wounded, and they are thrown into a spiritual and religious crisis as a result of the assault and church leaders' collusion.

Because the soul is the essence of what it is to be human and is intimately connected with life and the Giver of Life, soul wounds send the wounded into a very dark place. This book explores the soul wounds of women who have been sexually assaulted by a clergyperson and tells their stories of what has happened since the abusive relationship with the clergyperson ended.

But first, some helpful history.

POSSIBLE SYMPTOMS OF CLERGY SEXUAL ASSAULT

Dispirited	Insomnia
Withdrawal from others	Increased irritability
Impulsive crying	Listlessness
Depression	Exaggerated startle reflex
Nervousness	Inability to concentrate
Anxiety	Eating disorders
Self-mutilation	Alcohol or substance abuse
Suicidal Impulses	Drastic change in personality
Panic attacks	Uncontrollable shaking
Dazed	Feeling outside one's body
Visual hallucinations	Auditory hallucinations
Stomach aches, nausea	Compulsions or obsessions
Gastrointestinal upsets	Drastic weight gain or loss
Headaches	Bruising
Strained Relationships	Overachievement
Going into a trance	Disorientation
Various phobias	

- ✓ Memory disturbance (all the way to amnesia to fugue states)
- ✓ Difficulty understanding others
- ✓ Inability to perform daily tasks
- ✓ Inability to understand or participate in simple conversations
- ✓ Drastic change in appearance, such as dressing sexy or dowdy
- ✓ Morbid preoccupations with things such as death, abuse, suicide
- ✓ Strong negative reaction to being touched
- ✓ Sexual dysfunction such as: diminished sexual desire (all the way to asexuality), promiscuity, need for rape fantasies to achieve sexual excitement, inability to achieve orgasm
- ✓ Sexually transmitted diseases, unwanted pregnancy, yeast infections, vaginal/rectal tearing

Chapter 2

The History of Clergy Sexual Assault in the United States

Clergy sexual assault has only recently been recognized as an abuse of power. Prior to such recognition, neither the dynamics nor the damage done to the laborer were understood. This chapter explores the historical context of clergy sexual assault in the United States.

When I searched through old newspaper and magazine articles, the earliest published reference I found to clergy sexual assault was in 1872. This is not to say that clergy sexual assault of adult women did not take place before that. In 1850, Nathaniel Hawthorne wrote his well-known novel *The Scarlet Letter*,[21] which tells the story of Hester Prynne's "illicit" relationship with Rev. Arthur Dimmesdale, for which she was sentenced to wear a scarlet "A" on her chest so the world would know her sin.

Sexual assault of minorities has also been documented. Minority women, such as slaves and, later, sharecroppers, were often raped by slave or land owners. Native American women were raped by soldiers and missionaries. Native American children who had been sent to Christian boarding schools by the United States government in an attempt to expunge Native culture from the children and "civilize" them, were often

---

[21] Nathaniel Hawthorne, *The Scarlet Letter,* (New York, Bantam Dell, 2003).

sexually abused by the clergy and nuns who ran the boarding schools.[22] Although there is very little documentation of clergy sexually assaulting women prior to 1872, the reason is likely that those who recorded history did not believe such stories were worth recording, especially if the one abused was a woman or a child from a minority group.

1872

In the 1870s, the famous abolitionist, Rev. Henry Ward Beecher, brother to Harriet Beecher Stowe, was accused of having a "free love" relationship with Mrs. Elizabeth Tilton, a member of his congregation, Plymouth Church. Elizabeth had gone to Rev. Beecher for counsel after the death of her infant around 1868. A sexual relationship ensued. Eventually, Elizabeth told her husband about the relationship, first stating that it was a consensual love relationship and later that Rev. Beecher had made improper advances toward her.[23] Mr. Tilton agreed to keep the story quiet, but soon others in the community suspected that Rev. Beecher was guilty of infidelity and the story ultimately ran in Victoria Woodhull's weekly abolitionist newspaper.[24]

---

[22] Sharon Waxman, "Sioux Allege Abuse at Church Boarding Schools," *Washington Post,* June 2, 2003; Andrea Smith, "Soul Wound: The Legacy of Native American Schools," *Amnesty International Magazine*, March 26, 2007.

[23] Such a change in perspective is common for a laborer as time progresses. She begins processing the relationship and is able to recognize the manipulative manner in which she was groomed for the relationship and in which her vulnerabilities were exploited. Eventually, she comes to the realization that she was abused.

[24] "Beecher-Tilton Scandal," Brown University Library, n.d, http://library.brown.edu/exhibits/archive/RLCexhibit/beecher/beecherms.html, accessed on March 11, 2010.

When the story ran in the press, Mr. Tilton became upset and the leaders of Plymouth Church investigated the situation. As a result, they withdrew Mr. Tilton's membership and exonerated Rev. Beecher, issuing a report. A portion of this report follows:

> This man [Rev. Beecher] has been living in the clear light of noonday, before his people and before all men, a life of great Christian usefulness and incessant work. None have known him but to admire and love him. . . . Upon review of all the evidence, made with an earnest desire to find the truth, and to advise what truth and justice shall require, we feel bound to state that, in our judgment, the evidence relied on by the accuser utterly fails to sustain the charges made.[25]

Mr. Tilton, unhappy with the church's report, then sought justice by suing Rev. Beecher for committing adultery with his wife. The trial was covered by the press as Rev. Beecher was a prominent preacher and well liked. He was acquitted. Although his career was tarnished by the publicity, he continued in his ministerial position at Plymouth Church. However, after the trial, Mr. Tilton was unable to find employment due to his damaged reputation, and he eventually moved to Paris to start a new life. Elizabeth was "ostracized by Plymouth Church . . . [and] died in 1897, lonely and blind, at the

---

[25] Stephen Christianson, "Tilton v. Beecher: 1875," *Great American Trials* (2002), http://www.encyclopedia.com/doc/1G2-3498200091.html.

home of her daughter in Brooklyn."[26] This highly publicized case demonstrates that in the 1800s, society viewed clergy sexual assault as infidelity, and the woman involved faced the harshest penalty.

1970s

Beyond the Tilton-Beecher scandal of the 1870s, there is little printed evidence regarding so-called clergy "affairs" in the United States for roughly one hundred years. The next example is from 1971.

In that year, for the first time in Navy history, a chaplain was court-martialed on adultery charges. In the *Time* magazine article which reported the story, the Navy chaplain's sexual relationships with several officers' wives were referred to as "adultery" and an "affair," and the article's leading sentence was "It was a tawdry story."[27] The article went on to state that the American Baptist Convention declared the court-martial to be "an attempt at character defamation, emphatically contending that they [the American Baptist Convention] are the sole judges of the moral and spiritual qualifications of their ministers. To underscore its ire, the convention announced that it would send no more chaplains to the Navy until the Government formally recognized its claim."[28] Although the Navy viewed such behavior as suspect on the moral grounds of adultery, the American Baptist Convention was in denial concerning even that charge. Neither the Navy nor the Ameri-

---

[26] Ann-Janine Morey, "Blaming Women for the Sexually Abusive Male Pastor," *The Christian Century* 105 (2002): 867.
[27] "TRIALS: The Chaplain's Case," *Time* April 3, 1972, www.time.com/time/magazine/article/0,9171,903391,00.html.
[28] Ibid.

can Baptist Convention entertained the idea that the relationship was abusive. In addition, *Time* magazine's leading sentence sensationalized the story.

The following year, in 1972, a woman in Dallas filed an "$830,000 suit against her pastor, his bishop, and the Episcopal Diocese on the grounds of professional misconduct. The woman's husband also sued, contending the pastor was under satanic influence. The Texas Supreme Court threw out the case."[29] This case in Dallas was the earliest public record I was able to find which referred to such a relationship as "professional misconduct."

1980s and 1990s

In 1977, the Rev. Dr. Marie Fortune founded the Center for the Prevention of Sexual and Domestic Violence, which today is known as the FaithTrust Institute. The purpose of this organization is to advocate, educate, and address faith issues around sexual abuse and domestic violence. In 1983, Fortune received a phone call from a woman whose pastor had sexually harassed her. As more women began calling regarding harassment and assault by members of the clergy, the Center realized these women were being sexually victimized and isolated, and that this was a widespread problem.[30]

---

[29] Laurinda Keys, "Church Is No Longer Malpractice Sanctuary," *The Free Lance Star,* June 7, 1980. http://news.google.com/newspapers?nid=1298&dat=19800607&id=XOsQAAAAIBAJ&sjid=6osDAAAAIBAJ&pg=5649,966928.

[30] "FaithTrust Institute Hopes Religious Institutions Will Be Sanctuaries of Safety," *The Fig Tree,* November 2008. http://www.thefigtree.org/nov08/110108faithtrust.html.

About this same time, three important events happened that began to shift the country's perception of the clergy. First, in 1980, the case of *Nally v. Grace Community Church* was the first time a church was sued for malpractice in which the case was actually heard in court. Although the Dallas case of 1972 had been heard in court, the suit was filed on the grounds of professional misconduct not malpractice. Misconduct is a violation of a profession's ethical codes. Someone committing misconduct is usually disciplined by their professional organization. Clergy who commit misconduct are supposedly disciplined by their denomination. When the denomination fails to act, civil litigation might be filed.

Nally v. Grace Community Church was a malpractice suit. Malpractice is defined as failing to meet the basic level of competence required in one's profession. However, because clergy are not licensed professionals such as doctors, lawyers, psychologists, and social workers, they are only accountable to the religious standards of their denominations; the courts have no legal jurisdiction over them. Because clergy are not licensed by the state, and because the First Amendment of the Constitution specifies the separation of church and state, clergy malpractice suits rarely win in the courts.

Prior to *Nally v. Grace Community Church*, cases of malpractice brought against the church were typically dismissed due to First Amendment issues. Although *Nally v. Grace Community Church* was not a sexual misconduct case, it did open the doors for other clergy malpractice suits to be heard by the courts, including sexual misconduct. Still, such hearings tend to result in the court's ruling in favor of the church and the clergy.

The second event which began to shift the public's perception of the clergy took place in the mid-1980s, when the scandal of Catholic priests molesting children[31] and the ensuing cover-ups were widely covered by the media. This scandal began creating an awareness that the church could be a place of corruption and that some priests were dishonest men who hide behind the clergy collar.

The third event that contributed to the shift in perception concerning the clergy occurred in the late 1980s and early 1990s. During this time, three well-known televangelists—Marvin Gorman, James Bakker, and Jimmy Swaggart—publicly confessed their sexual infidelities.[32] During this same period, reports began to surface that the faith healing some televangelists practiced was demonstrably fraudulent. The confessions of sexual infidelity, combined with the fraudulent faith-healing claims, created a media circus that was virtually impossible to ignore and provided fodder for comedians and other forms of entertainment. In 1992, Paramount Pictures released *Leap of Faith*[33] starring Steve Martin as Jonas, a fraudulent faith healer. Throughout the movie, Jonas seeks to "seduce" a woman he has met while passing through town.

In response to this paradigm shift, people began to organize and advocate, and policies began to change. By 1986, Minnesota and Wisconsin became the first two states to pass legislation making it a criminal offense for clergy to sexually

---

[31] Although stories of victims who were boys made the news, there were also many girls who were victimized by Catholic priests. Those stories are perceived to be less shocking and, therefore, are not as readily publicized.

[32] John Dart, "Denies Takeover Attempt: Issued Warning about Bakker, Swaggart Says," *Los Angeles Times*, March 25, 1987; "Swaggart Plans to Step Down," *The New York Times,* October, 15, 1991.

[33] *Leap of Faith,* directed by Richard Pearce (1992, Hollywood, CA: Paramount Pictures, 2003), DVD.

exploit members of their congregations.[34] In 1989, Marie Fortune published *Is Nothing Sacred?* and Peter Rutter published *Sex in the Forbidden Zone.* Both books addressed the damaging nature of clergy sexual misconduct.[35] Also that year, Barbara Blaine founded Survivors Network for those Abused by Priests (SNAP), the first support group for survivors of clergy sexual abuse. These policies and books, along with the formation of SNAP, gave victims, therapists, and clergy language to attach to clergy sexual misconduct and abuse, and defined the damage that occurs when someone is abused. In response to this new awareness and the fact that churches were being sued for misconduct, denominations began taking so-called "clergy affairs" more seriously by reexamining their ethics, writing new policies, and taking out malpractice insurance.

The New Millennium

Newspaper stories from the 1990s and the first years of the twenty-first century sometimes refer to clergy sexual assault as sexual misconduct. Yet, there were still many instances of such relationships being called "consensual sex" or "an affair." Several newspaper stories from the early 2000s mention that clergy sexual abuse of adults, primarily women, happens more frequently than clergy sexual abuse of children. One of these articles was based on a report by the National Review Board, which was established by the United States

---

[34] 1985 Wisconsin Act 275; Minnesota Statute 1986 c 372 s 1.
[35] Marie Fortune, *Is Nothing Sacred?* (Cleveland: United Church Press, 1999); Peter Rutter, *Sex in the Forbidden Zone: When Men in Power—Therapists, Doctors, Clergy, Teachers, and Others—Betray Women's Trust* (Los Angeles: Jeremy P. Tarcher, 1989).

Conference of Catholic Bishops to prevent clergy sexual abuse of minors in the church.[36]

In 2007, the Baptist General Convention of Texas began publishing on its website the names of clergy who were registered sex offenders and were currently on staff at their affiliated churches.[37] To be a registered sex offender, the clergyperson had to have a conviction of rape, child molestation, or sexual battery. In 2009, Baylor University published the largest scientific study to date on clergy sexual misconduct with adults.[38] In 2011, John Jay College of Criminal Justice at City University published a study on the causes and context of clergy sexual abuse in the U.S. Catholic Church. This study found that 70 percent of priests who had abused a minor "had also had sexual behavior with adults. The majority of priest-abusers did not specialize in abusing 'particular types of victims.'"[39]

Although the paradigm began to shift from "clergy affairs" to "clergy misconduct" about twenty years ago and some denominations began to develop policies to prevent and respond to clergy sexual assault, sometimes such relationships are still treated as consensual or as an affair by the congregation, the denomination, and the press.

In the following section, I introduce the eighteen participants interviewed for this book. Of those eighteen, five of them were sexually assaulted between 1976 and 1989, three in the

---

36 Jerry Filteau, "Report Says Clergy Sexual Abuse Brought 'Smoke of Satan' into Church," *Catholic News Service*, February 27, 2004.
37 John Hall, "BGCT Posts Clergy Registered Sex Offenders," *Baptist General Convention of Texas*, June 6, 2007.
38 Audrey Barrick, "Survey Reveals Prevalence of Clergy Sexual Misconduct," *The Christian Post*, September 11, 2009.
39 "Causes and Context Report Released on Clergy Sexual Abuse of Minors," *Catholic Sentinel*, May 18, 2011.

1990s and ten in the 2000s. As you read each synopsis, try to place the women in their historical clergy sexual assault context. See if you notice any improvements through the years in the manner in which laborers have been treated when news of their assault was disclosed.

SECTION II

The Laborers

You gain strength, courage, and confidence by every experience in which you really stop to look fear in the face. You are able to say to yourself, "I lived through this horror. I can take the next thing that comes along."

—Eleanor Roosevelt

Chapter 3

Dark Night of the Soul

Prior to their assault, all the laborers in this research had a history of active involvement in congregational life and had spiritual disciplines which they practiced regularly. Most identified heavily with their denomination to the extent that some had very limited exposure to people outside their denomination. Laborers' faith, their relationship with God, and their congregational involvement were means they used to define themselves. As a result of their sexual assault, most underwent an identity crisis. For every laborer this crisis included the loss of their church family. Many lost friends and some lost husbands. Some close relationships with parents, siblings, children, and extended family members became strained. A few lost jobs, and one laborer's husband lost his position in a religious setting. Those with a religious career lost it despite having completed considerable schooling toward that career. Some lost dreams of a future religious career. Some lost their sense of purpose for existing. A few kept their assault to themselves so as not to burden their loved ones.

In addition, some experienced depression, PTSD, suicidal ideation, psychosis, substance abuse, and self-harm, such as cutting. Not only did the laborers have to work through their many losses; they also had to come to terms with being betrayed by a member of the clergy and, in many cases, by their denomination's inability to reach out to them in a supportive, just, and healing manner.

Most people are able to turn to their faith for support in times of crisis. But the majority of laborers were not initially able to do so. One reason was the betrayal and collusion they experienced on the part of religious leaders. These leaders represented to the laborers sacred concepts such as God, compassion, justice, and reconciliation. When the leaders failed to respond to the assault in a godly manner, this contributed to the laborer's faith crisis and often prompted stronger trauma symptoms. Such symptoms were commonly triggered by exposure to religious or spiritual symbols, such as entering a church and having a panic attack, or seeing a religious picture and experiencing a flashback—a memory that surfaces unexpectedly and is so vivid, it seems the remembered event is occurring in the present.

In many cases, the laborers experienced such severe faith crises that a period of atheism, agnosticism, or spiritual numbness resulted. A period of atheism seemed, for the most part, to be an early stage of the rebirthing process. However, the agnosticism and spiritual numbness sometimes lasted for years. Laborers are different from most who self-identify as atheists and agnostics in that they do not make an intellectual choice to hold these beliefs; rather, such beliefs are a direct result of clergy sexual assault and denominational and congregational collusion. Unlike self-proclaimed atheists and agnostics, most laborers find both these labels and their spiritual numbness intolerable.

For the laborers in this book, the faith crisis is similar in many regards to the dark night of the soul, first identified by St. John of the Cross, a sixteenth-century Carmelite friar and Spanish mystic. The dark night of the soul is a phase in spiritual development in which spiritual practices lose meaning for the faithful and it feels as if God has withdrawn from one's life.

John experienced the dark night of the soul while he was imprisoned by his religious order, the Carmelites.

Although John of the Cross had the approval of the Spanish Papal Nuncio to carry out reforms in his order, he was imprisoned by his religious superiors who disapproved of these reforms. For nine months, he was locked in a damp, six-by-ten-foot cell with a two-inch opening high in the wall which let in a small amount of light for a portion of each day. John was left in such squalor with little to eat and was flogged periodically. His wounds, left untreated, became infested with maggots. For a long time he had no change of clothing and wore only his blood-stained garments. After escaping, John of the Cross wrote his famous book, *Dark Night of the Soul.*

John's experience is not dissimilar to that of laborers who have also been thrown into the spiritual void of the dark night of the soul due to their severe treatment by religious leaders.

John of the Cross writes regarding the dark night:

> The afflictions and constraints of the will are now very great likewise, and of such a kind that they sometimes transpierce the soul with a sudden remembrance of the evils in the midst of which it finds itself, and with the uncertainty of finding a remedy for them. And to this is added the remembrance of a time of prosperity now past; for as a rule souls that enter this night have had many consolations from God, and have rendered Him many services, and it causes them the greater grief to see that they are far removed from that happiness, and unable to enter into it. This was also described by Job who had had experi-

> ence of it, in these words: "I, who was wont to be wealthy and rich, am suddenly undone and broken to pieces; He hath taken me by my neck; He hath broken me and set me up for his mark to wound me; He hath compassed me roundabout with his lances; He hath wounded all my loins; He hath not spared; He hath poured out my bowels on the earth; He hath broken me with wound upon wound; He hath assailed me as a strong giant; I have sewed sackcloth upon my skin and covered my flesh with ashes; my face is become swollen with weeping and mine eyes are blinded."[40]

The words of John of the Cross and Job are quite similar to those of the laborers, who often were unable to reestablish a connection with the Divine despite an intense longing to do so. This is demonstrated by the words of Yasmine, a laborer from the Middle East who will be more fully introduced in the next chapter:

> I ended up empty and void. I don't really know what the meaning of my life is, and spiritually, there is no God, and sometimes I would feel there is no point in living. My life was for God, and later on there is no meaning to my life. I started to stop believing in everything, and so the tunnel was dark. There was no light. I don't want to be an atheist, but at the same time, I don't have op-

---

[40] St. John of the Cross, *Dark Night of the Soul,* trans. E. Allison Peers (New York: Image Books, 1990), 108-109.

> tions. I don't have a relationship with God. God doesn't love me. He doesn't want me. How do you find God? Without this, I will never find peace. I don't trust myself anymore. I have lost not only the belief in God but the belief in myself. The belief in my integrity. The belief that one day I am going to be a good woman. I don't know what I am.

Such spiritual isolation and anguish are hallmarks of the dark night of the soul. In the Christian mystical tradition, Jesus is perceived as having gone through the dark night when he was dying on the cross and cried out, "My God, my God, why have you forsaken me?" (Mark 15:34b). In his excruciating pain and anguish, he felt spiritually abandoned.

The dark night of the soul is not limited to Christianity; it is found throughout the world's religious traditions, although it is known by different names. For example, Sufism, the mystical branch of Islam, notes a similar experience on the path toward union with God. Farīd ud-Dīn Aṭṭār, a Sufi theoretician, writes, "You will lose what you have considered valuable, but eventually you'll hear the voice you've most wanted to hear saying, '*Yes. Come in.*'"[41]

In many indigenous cultures which practice Shamanism, the phenomenon of the dark night is known as soul loss. According to this understanding, soul loss occurs to each of us as we go through life and experience frightening situations. At such a time, a small piece of the soul splinters off and becomes lost as a way of protecting the individual from harm. Usually,

---

[41] Coleman Barks, trans., *Rumi: The Book of Love*, trans. Coleman Barks, (San Francisco: HarperCollins, 2003), 62.

we do not notice small losses of our soul. For example, a toddler crying at night because she is afraid of the dark may lose a small piece of her soul and never miss it. However, when something devastating occurs, a large portion of the soul is splintered and the person may sink into darkness; their behavior changes drastically, preventing healing even though they may take action to try to heal. For instance, a man involved in a serious car accident may not be able to remember the crash and may change his behavior and refuse to ride in a car. In Shamanic practice, it is believed he has lost a considerable portion of the soul. In such cases, the shaman or shamanic practitioner is called upon to journey to the spirit world to retrieve pieces of the splintered soul and return them to their owner. These splintered pieces have remained innocent of the traumatic event because they were lost prior to it. When the pieces are reunited with the person, the person again remembers the time of innocence prior to the trauma. This innocence enables healing to progress.

In Buddhism, the dark night of the soul is experienced as an aspect of the Four Noble Truths: (1) Suffering exists. (2) There is a cause to suffering. (3) Suffering can end. (4) The way to end suffering is to follow the Eightfold Path. The Eightfold Path includes, appropriately enough, eight factors: right view, right intention, right speech, right thinking, right action, right livelihood, right effort, right mindfulness, and right concentration. When practiced, these eight factors enable the practitioner to realize that true spirituality is born of suffering, and they become the practical steps for ending one's suffering. The Four Noble Truths and the Eightfold Path were the primary teachings of Buddha and provide a practice designed to transform suffering into enlightenment.

For many of the women whose stories are shared in this book, it seemed that moving beyond the dark night was the most difficult feat of their assault experience. At the time of our interviews, three women said they had come to a place of contentment and fulfillment. Some said they were close. Yet the majority stated they had not felt spiritual since the assault and were still struggling with finding meaning in their life, finding a spiritual practice, or finding a meaningful career despite, in some cases, many years having passed.

Perhaps their difficulty in healing is in part because, unlike St. John of the Cross, who, after his imprisonment, was accepted within the monastic community and was able to resume his monastic reforms and to found new monasteries, many laborers have not found support within their religious tradition. Rather, they have felt alienated by their denomination as they struggle to establish new work and a new sense of meaning.

In addition, most religious institutions and faith traditions draw a fairly rigid box around what constitutes orthodoxy and acceptable spiritual practices, and around what is deemed heretical, cultic, or satanic. These rigid boxes create a quandary for a woman who finds herself isolated from her religious tradition and desires spiritual nourishment. Where can she find spiritual guidance if her tradition has marginalized her? How does she venture outside that tradition if she has been taught that salvation is found only within its bounds?

Laborers whose spiritual healing seemed to have progressed the furthest had taken steps to change the things they found unacceptable in their lives, and were vocal self-advocates regarding their clergy sexual assault. They had carved out a spiritual path that worked for them, had told their story repeatedly, had supported other laborers, and had become engaged in life. In order to do these things, they had struggled to overcome certain obstacles. However, in their determination to overcome such obstacles, and with each telling of their story and each woman they helped, it seemed they received a portion of healing in return.

Those laborers who found both supportive clergy and a supportive congregation within their denomination tended to progress to a deeper spirituality within their tradition than they had experienced before the assault, and their spiritual closeness with God was strengthened, much as John of the Cross experienced. Similarly, laborers who no longer identified with their tradition but had explored spirituality outside it tended to have moved beyond their dark night to a place of spiritual fulfillment, although this place looked somewhat different from the tradition they had left. In spite of this difference, they reported feeling a stronger connection to Spirit than they had prior to their assault.

Whatever direction the spiritual journey took, it required time and perseverance to move beyond the dark night toward a spiritually satisfying life. Each progressing laborer's spiritual life was fluid, ever changing and unfolding as she discovered new avenues, new experiences, and new depths to her understanding of Spirit, the world, and humanity. Yet some laborers still struggle with finding a way out of the darkness.

Thomas Moore writes in *Dark Nights of the Soul* that the dark night is an opportunity similar to that of an embryo awaiting birth, and his recommendation for moving through the dark night is to become similar to the human embryo. He urges one to try to rest in the darkness as an embryo rests within the womb, awaiting birth.

> When you sense that your dark night is one of pregnancy and oceanic return, you could react accordingly and be still. Watch and wonder. Take the human embryo as your model. Assume the fetal position, emotionally and intellectually. Be silent. Float in your darkness as if it were the waters of the womb, and give up trying to fight your way and make sense of it.[42]

All the laborers experienced this darkness, and each spoke of her desire to make the world a better place—even those laborers still floating within the dark embryonic fluid. Yes, some in the darkness felt stuck. Yes, some in the darkness felt like seeking revenge. Yes, some in the darkness were enraged. But underneath these normal feelings of victimization was an inner resolve to be more compassionate. The English word "compassion" comes from the Latin word *compatior*, which means "to suffer with." Truly, the wisdom of compassion was birthed in all the laborers in response to their suffering.

---

[42] Thomas Moore, *Dark Nights of the Soul: A Guide to Finding Your Way through Life's Ordeals*, (New York: Gotham Books, 2004), 12.

Chapter 4

Meet the Laborers

The primary research in this book was based on eighteen interviews with laborers. At the time of the interviews (June 2010 through March 2011), a few of the laborers had reached a place of rebirth, although most continue to push their way through the birthing process of becoming. Some are gripped daily by the sheer intensity of their labor pains. Yet all the women exhibited inner strength, perseverance, a desire for wholeness, a search for meaning, and a greater capacity for compassion. This chapter outlines the demographics of the laborers, along with the grooming and assaults they experienced, and introduces the reader to each woman.

Eleven different religious denominations were represented. Four participants had been assaulted by Evangelical Lutheran Church in America (ELCA) pastors and four by Roman Catholic priests. Two were assaulted by Lutheran Church-Missouri Synod (LCMS) pastors. The remaining assaults involved one clergyperson from each of the following denominations: Conservative Grace Brethren, Cooperative Baptist Fellowship, Episcopal, Independent Baptist, Reform Judaism, Seventh Day Adventist, Unitarian Universalist, and United Methodist. One participant was a Muslim who was converting to Christianity at the time of her assault. One woman was assaulted by a female clergyperson.

Denominations Represented

The laborers in this play were abused by clergy from the following denominations (the number that follows the denomination indicates the number of laborers who were abused by a clergyperson from that denomination. No two women in my research were abused by the same clergyperson.

Conservative Grace Brethren (1)

Cooperative Baptist Fellowship (1)

ELCA Lutheran (4)

Episcopal (1)

Independent Baptist (1)

Missouri Synod Lutheran (2)

Reform Judaism (1)

Roman Catholic (4)

Seventh Day Adventist (1)

Unitarian Universalist (1)

United Methodist (1)

Although the laborers in this study represented eleven denominations from three different religions, clergy sexual assault takes place in all religions and denominations of the world. The sample used in this research was primarily Christian because the sample was sought in the United States, which is 78.4 percent Christian.[43] This sample also contains a high percentage of Catholics and Lutherans. This by no means implies that clergy sexual assault is primarily a Catholic or Lutheran problem. There are several reasons for the high numbers of Catholic and Lutheran responses. First, Catholicism is the largest denomination in the United States.[44] Second, Catholic survivors of childhood clergy sexual abuse have organized several grassroots support organizations in which laborers also have found support. Because this network is already in place, many Catholic laborers are on their mailing lists and received information through these organizations regarding this research opportunity. Third, when the numbers of ELCA and Missouri Synod Lutherans in the U.S. are combined, they become the fourth-largest religious group in the country.[45] Finally, I used to own a website that was directed at Lutheran laborers, and I sent out invitations to participate in this research via my mailing list; though not all the Lutherans who participated in this research were on the mailing list, some did connect with this study via that route.

The laborers lived in twelve U.S. states, located in four geographic regions of the country. Those states in order of

---

[43]"Major Religious Traditions in the U.S.," *The Pew Forum on Religion and Public Life.*, http://religions.pewforum.org/reports, accessed September 25, 2011.

[44] "Largest 25 Denominations/Communions from the 2011 Yearbook of American and Canadian Churches," *Hartford Institute for Religious Research*, http://hirr.hartsem.edu/research/fastfacts/fast_facts.html.

[45] Ibid.

participant prevalence are Texas, Illinois, Minnesota, Ohio, California, Indiana, Florida, Massachusetts, Missouri, Nebraska, South Carolina, and Vermont. One laborer lived in the Middle East. A laborer's place of residence at the time of the interview was not necessarily where her assault had occurred.

The laborers ranged in age from twenty to fifty-five at the time of the assault, with the average age being thirty-four. Sixteen of the participants were Caucasian, one was African American, and one was Middle Eastern. All women were assaulted by American clergy except the Middle Eastern woman, who was assaulted by a Middle Eastern clergyman.

All the clergy offenders had college educations, and all but two held master's degrees. One of these two had attended his denomination's Church Practorium in place of seminary, which his denomination views as equivalent to a seminary degree. The other man attended seminary but did not graduate. He lied to his denominational leaders by telling them he had graduated, and over the years he had been promoted to a high level in his denomination despite lacking the proper educational credentials. Two of the clergy held doctoral degrees, one in education and one in social ethics.

The length of time since the abusive relationship ended ranged at the time of the interviews from one and a half years to thirty-one years, with the average time being fourteen years. Six of the women mentioned having experienced prior sexual victimization, such as rape, incest, or child molestation. Most did not recognize what happened to them as abusive until after the clergy sexual relationship ended. This is common with women who have been victimized by clergy because the women tend to blame themselves and exonerate the "man of God." For some, it took between many months and many years after the relationship for them to name it as abusive. All had sought counseling due to the assault, though some waited a period of years to do so. One reported that she received counseling for "verbal and emotional abuse" because, in her words, "in the late 1970s, clergy sexual abuse of adult women was not something therapists were aware of or thinking of."

Fifteen of these eighteen cases were reported to denominational leaders, while the one involving an independent church was reported to congregational leaders. Of those sixteen cases, one pastor is currently serving a forty-year prison sentence. Seven pastors were removed from their position; however, most, if not all, retained their full pension, some retained their clergy credentials, and some presently serve in volunteer capacities in congregations.

The Episcopal priest transferred his ordination to the Anglican Mission in America. One of the Lutheran Church–Missouri Synod pastors was forced to retire but maintains his title. One ELCA pastor was asked to resign, but no paperwork was filed regarding his history of assault; he continues his ministry in the denomination as a music minister. The Cooperative Baptist Fellowship pastor continues employment in new ministries outside his denomination. Another ELCA pastor was removed from the clergy roster for a few years but then was reinstated, and the laborer he had assaulted was never notified by the denomination. The Unitarian Universalist minister, one Roman Catholic priest, and one other ELCA pastor were allowed to retain their ordained status. Two of these were moved to new congregations, and the other received a promotion.

All the laborers who had careers in the church lost them as a result of the assault.

The Laborers

The eighteen women in this research have varying ways of describing their assault, ranging from rape to "love" relationships and everything in between. In all cases, what transpired was clergy sexual assault. This is because in a clergy-congregant relationship, the clergyperson holds all the power, making the congregant not truly capable of giving consent. It is similar to a teacher-student relationship. The teacher is responsible for teaching and mentoring the student. The student looks up to the teacher and trusts the teacher to do his or her job by holding the best interests of the student in mind. Students do not expect to be propositioned by their teachers, just as congregants do not expect to be propositioned by their clergyperson. In addition, when a senior clergyperson or supervising clergyperson assaults a member of the clergy on his staff or whom he is mentoring, this, too, constitutes clergy sexual assault because the senior clergyperson holds all the power.

Most of the eighteen participants have been given pseudonyms. That is the only information that has been changed.

Each laborer's introduction describes grooming techniques used against her and how much time had passed since her assault at the time of the interview. The laborers are introduced according to how long ago their assaults occurred, with the most recent assaults described last. The time frame is provided in each case to give the reader a sense of progress, or lack thereof, that has been made by religious institutions in responding to clergy sexual assault.

Valerie

Valerie had a full-time career in the church at the time of her clergy rape. She suppressed the rape and continued working in various parishes. As the years passed, she began to hear rumblings in the church about a number of priests' inappropriate behavior; this troubled her. She eventually stopped believing the teachings of the church and questioned who her Higher Power was. Several times, she tried to share her spiritual struggles with various priests she thought would be sympathetic to her revelation of rape and able to help her. Yet, time and again her belief that the priests would be capable of discerning her struggles concerning what she believed proved wrong. She felt that if they could not even hear her *spiritual* struggles, she *certainly* could not tell them about being raped by a priest.

Eventually, Valerie became involved with SNAP, the group that had been organized to help survivors who had been abused in childhood by members of the clergy. Through meeting people at SNAP, she was finally able to disclose what had happened to her, and she learned that the rape had not been her fault. It had been an abuse of power. This was very healing to her.

Today, Valerie continues her involvement with SNAP by organizing events and being present with men and women as they share their stories of clergy abuse. She still struggles with her spirituality and wrestles with the concept of her Higher Power. Valerie was raped thirty-five years ago.

Sharon

Sharon went to Catholic grade school, high school, college, and graduate school. All of her family and friends were Catholic. She had a vibrant faith and talked to God all the time. Sharon took a position as a Director of Religious Education several hours from the city in which she had been raised. She found her position fulfilling and was enthused by her work. However, she was lonely and felt isolated. During this time, Sharon was introduced to a priest stationed as a chaplain at a nearby Army base. Sharon and the priest started to see each other socially. (Although he was not Sharon's priest, this incident is considered to be clergy sexual assault because Catholic priests are not allowed to marry and Sharon trusted that his intentions were to have a platonic relationship.) Soon the priest began to hold her hand and put his arm around her. Then he began pressuring her to have sex. Sharon had been raised to be a "good Catholic girl" and did not want to give in. The priest worked to break down her moral and religious objections. As time went on, the priest's advances became bolder, and after three months of resistance, Sharon surrendered. Later, Sharon learned that she was the seventh woman this priest had had a sexual relationship with; he had joined the Army in order to travel the world and hook up with women at each base. He eventually applied for a transfer to Asia and left Sharon feeling emotionally used, in addition to having been sexually abused.

From the time of the relationship onward, Sharon became disillusioned in her faith and did not feel she could continue her career in the church with any sense of honesty. She tried to disclose what had happened to a close Catholic friend, but the friend shut her out. Sharon was afraid to tell her conservative Catholic parents. So she carried her secret, which caused her much pain, guilt, and shame, for more than thirty years. She struggled with finding a new career and pursued a second master's in counseling. After Sharon had completed the course work for a Ph.D. in counseling psychology, she decided that counseling was not a good career fit for her. She then completed a master's of fine arts degree in ceramics and art history.

Today, Sharon owns her own art-related business. Only recently did she realize that her relationship with the priest was never an *equal* one, and that the priest had employed grooming techniques with the intention of sexual assault from the very beginning of the relationship. Sharon still struggles spiritually because of the alienation she felt from the church and her church friends. Her assault happened thirty-two years ago.

Dee

When Dee was five years old, her mother died and her paternal grandmother came to live with them. Over the years, her grandmother told stories of their family history.

One such story was revealed to Dee when she was preparing for a school test and mentioned some of the content she was studying—the famous author Harriet Beecher Stowe and her book *Uncle Tom's Cabin*. Dee's grandmother replied, "My pa was related to her through marriage." Later, her grandmother told that in 1875, her family had moved as far west as the train would take them.

When Dee was ten, her grandmother "dragged" her to church, as she tells it, saying they had "been heathen long enough." Dee became active in her congregation and took leadership roles in the church as an adult. After her own children had grown, Dee moved out of state, taking a four-year position as the president of her denomination's women's group. While holding this position, she began to have flashbacks of being raped twice as an adult by the pastor of her home congregation. She eventually came forward with other victims from the congregation and participated in a denominational trial. Dee's denomination paid for counseling, which she found helpful. After the trial, she finished her term as president, returned to her hometown, and was shunned by people from her congregation. She tried to attend another nearby congregation of her denomination but felt she did not fit in. Dee left the church altogether and only goes now if she needs to attend a funeral or a wedding.

Five years after the trial, Dee was visiting her daughter and began to read Marie Fortune's *Is Nothing Sacred?* In the introduction, she read that Harriet Beecher Stowe's brother, the Rev. Henry Ward Beecher, had committed clergy sexual misconduct with Elizabeth Tilton and others. This prompted Dee to hypothesize that perhaps it was shame over the Beecher-Tilton scandal that caused her family to leave New York in the 1870s and move as far west as possible. She wondered if her grandmother knew "the secret" or if it had been silenced with the westward move.

Dee also wondered if "what goes around, comes around" and if someone in the next generation of kin had also been sexually abused by a clergyperson since the family shame of Rev. Beecher's abuse of power seemed so intense. Neither was Dee the only person in her immediate family who was abused by clergy. The pastor who raped her also sexually abused her grown daughter. As a senior citizen, Dee enrolled in a university and pursued Women's Studies. She says that doing so allowed her "the platform, permission, and support to speak on her personal experiences of clergy rape."

Today, Dee believes that "this soul destroying, soul murder, spiritual abuse can only stop when we break the silence and expose the evil by refusing to be part of the shame and collusion of clergy sexual abuse." She volunteers as a mentor for women who have been sexually assaulted by a clergyperson. She has been able to tailor a spiritually fulfilling life drawing from a variety of sources. Her rape took place twenty-five years ago.

Susan

Susan was about to graduate from a Christian college and was planning on attending seminary when she was raped by the college chaplain who had been her mentor. At seminary, she was again sexually assaulted, this time by another student. When she shared that information with a seminary professor, she was told that if she pursued it, it would be his word against hers and that he would be the one believed and she would be kicked out of seminary. The professor's response to her assault caused Susan to bury memories of the rape by her mentor, the college chaplain. Eventually, a bishop was elected to her state who wanted to weed out clergy offenders. Susan disclosed her rape. The pastor was stripped of his credentials, but all support for Susan on the part of the bishop ended at that point.

After graduating from seminary with her master's of divinity degree and serving several parishes, Susan completed a second master's, in mental health counseling. She enlisted in the Navy, where she was assigned a supervisor who turned out to be abusive. She filed a complaint and was told it was his word against hers. When she left the Armed Services, she was called to serve as an intentional interim pastor at a parish whose previous pastor had been a pedophile and molested multiple young boys in the congregation. Shortly after serving this parish, Susan went on disability for PTSD, which had invaded her life to such an extent that she was unable to work. Although she receives veterans assistance and social security disability, she receives no disability benefits from her denomination. In order to keep her clergy credentials with the denomination, Susan was told she needed to take an IQ test. This infuriated her and she fought for her right not to be subjected to something so irrelevant to her situation. At the time she was applying for disability, the pastor who had raped her was reinstated as a member of the clergy. Susan was not informed of this by the denomination.

Recently, Susan has enrolled in an online doctorate of education program in pastoral counseling. She still struggles with PTSD and anxiety on a regular basis and continues on disability. Susan was raped twenty-four years ago.

Rosa

Rosa grew up a "good Catholic girl," but due to being abused as a child by several of her brothers, she had a shaky faith. At eighteen, she had a numinous experience which made her realize that God was there for her. She continued in that faith while spending many hours visiting a local priest for counseling. She then moved away and worked hard to heal from her traumatic childhood and youth, employing the services of another therapist. After four and a half years of counseling and group therapy, Rosa felt she was in "a pretty good place." But the bottom fell out when her attempts to reconcile with her mother failed. While feeling rejected by her mother, she was also devastated by the breakup of a romantic relationship. So she turned to the priest who had counseled her before. After ten years of supporting her, he took advantage of her vulnerability, crossing the ethical line and being sexually intimate with her. After several such encounters, Rosa's confusion and disbelief woke her to the reality of what the priest was doing. She became suicidal and returned to her former therapist.

The priest who abused Rosa was from an order of Trappist monks from a monastery outside her town. Rosa got the courage to file a lawsuit, and as a result, the monastery gave Rosa a small settlement. The monastery termed the abuse "alleged" and settled out of court. The priest was forced to leave the monastery as the abbot did his best to push the entire matter under the carpet. Not much of an apology was made, nor was any further support offered to Rosa, though she states that no amount of money could ever make up for the devastating losses she had suffered at the hands of the priest. Later, Rosa turned to the monastery during tough times as a single parent, but the abbot refused to help, telling her that the settlement was all that she would get from them.

Rosa has struggled with PTSD and numerous stress-related health conditions due to the priest's sexual assault. She is unable to work at all, much less full-time. Relationships are very difficult for her due to her lack of trust in others, and she has lost dozens of friends, employers, and family relationships due to the self-blame, shame, and isolation brought on by the priest's actions. Her life since the abuse has been one of isolation and struggle, even for basic survival. She has shared her secret with only a few of her family because she fears most of them will not understand or support her if she tells them everything.

Life continues to be "a chaotic mess" as she works to manage depression which was worsened years ago by medication prescribed by her physician. Rosa's biggest heartbreak over the exploitation is that her only son has had to suffer due to her brokenness, and that he has missed out on so much life because of it. She has done many things to recover, but trusting God and others is a constant battle. Rosa looks forward to having a life free of debilitating pain. She works to manage it all with "one little glimmer of that light called hope"—hope that she can trust God, life, and others once again. Her assault happened twenty-two years ago.

Laurie

Laurie worked as a youth minister and had plans to attend seminary. All she ever wanted to do with her life was to be a pastor. She loved her job and was looking forward to her future. Then one day when she was dressed in yellow, she walked past the pastor and heard him say, "I want to peel you like a banana." Laurie thought the comment was inappropriate.

After that incident, he invited her to his house when his wife and children were not home, although at the time, Laurie did not know they were out of town. When she arrived, he gave her a glass of wine and she noticed a book on the table opened to some nude art. She thought the art must be something he had seen on his travels. He asked her to look at the book, and asked if the pictures made her feel uncomfortable. He put his hand under her sweatshirt and began rubbing her back. He then walked her to his bedroom where he removed her sweatshirt and held her for what seemed to Laurie like an eternity. He said, “What I am doing could ruin my ministry.”

Another time, Laurie was riding in his family van after a church youth ballgame. He stopped at a rest stop along the scenic highway and walked her to the backseat where he removed her pants, got on top of her, and touched her sexually. As this was happening, she was thinking, “He’s my boss. He’s vital to my ordination. How can I stop this?”

Laurie did manage to escape and get home. After this assault, she began drinking more than she ever had before. A short time later, she packed her bags, left the state, and moved in with a family member. She never shared information about the assault with her family, though they inquired about the abrupt change in the direction of her life. Eventually, she did disclose what had happened to church officials, and the press ran a story with a headline about “consensual sex.” She questioned the bishop about the word “consensual,” but was told it had to be used because she was an adult, not a child.

Today, Lauric still struggles with the loss of the career she felt she had always wanted. Her assault occurred twenty years ago.

Nancy

Nancy was married with children, was very involved in the church, and had plans to go to seminary, when her assault occurred. After the pastor had left the congregation and an interim pastor had been called, Nancy disclosed to him what had happened to her and found him to be unsupportive. The abusive pastor’s wife worked in the bishop’s office, Nancy’s complaint was covered up, and today no paperwork exists regarding the charge. Nancy talked to a lawyer about suing the church. However, the bishop's office began "playing games" with the paperwork the lawyer requested, and that, combined with the possibility of media coverage if the case went to trial, prompted Nancy to drop the suit. As a whole, she found her entire denomination unsupportive and collusive.

While all this was taking place, Nancy did not want her children to be without a church, so she found a new one to attend, in a different denomination. This congregation's clergy supported her. However, Nancy struggled and continues to struggle with the concept of church.

Today, Nancy works as a nurse and is back in school, planning to obtain a master's in nursing. From time to time, she thinks of attending seminary, but isn't sure she could do the "church community thing." Her assault occurred twenty years ago.

Amy

Amy was married with three children when she began seeing her pastor for counseling and shared with him that she was a survivor of early childhood sexual abuse. He was only the second person she had ever told. At the end of the session during which she shared that information, the pastor was adamant that she look him in the eyes, although she wasn't comfortable doing so. Despite his persistence, she never did look at him directly. She sat in the chair with her head down as he said, "Amy, I think you are a highly sexually charged woman, and what a blessing you are to your husband."

From that point on, he was sexually inappropriate and manipulative with her. But he also became important in Amy's life because of the role he was playing in her processing of her abusive past. When another woman in the church came forward stating that the pastor had crossed ethical boundaries with her, Amy told her husband what had been happening with the pastor. She then came forward with her story as well, and the pastor was removed from his position. Amy was told that had she not come forward, the pastor would have only received a "slap on the wrist." After coming forward, Amy's life fell apart and she was unable to function; she could not care for herself or her children. She moved in with a friend, who cared for her, and eventually she and her husband divorced.

Today Amy still struggles with the effects of the abuse and with her spirituality. Her abuse happened twelve years ago.

Willow

At the time of Willow's abuse, she was actively involved in her church. She describes the time directly prior to the abuse as the happiest of her adult life. She was married and had two children living at home. The assaultive relationship began when she sought counseling from her pastor and, in the course of counseling, believed she had fallen in love with him. After she had endured this manipulative "love" relationship for several years, he abruptly ended the relationship and she, in turn, reported him to her bishop. She reached out to her congregation and then to her denomination by doing an interview on clergy sexual assault with the denominational magazine. Despite her efforts at reaching out to her church, she has continually been marginalized.

Willow has talked with others in the congregation, learning there were other women who were sexually victimized by this pastor, yet she is the only one who came forward to the bishop's office. The denomination did pay for counseling, and her counselor helped with spiritual healing. Willow is still not accepted by her denomination. From time to time, she is still harassed by former congregants, despite the fact that eleven years have passed since the assaultive relationship ended.

Tabitha

Tabitha was involved in her congregation and viewed the other congregants as her family. Her pastor abused her while he was counseling her. At the time, she was married and had three children who were young adults. After she was abused, several victims in her congregation came forward with stories of clergy sexual abuse. Tabitha watched the other victims being shunned by the congregation and decided that when she came forward, she would hire a lawyer and file a civil lawsuit. When she did so, she was asked to leave the church. She became depressed, her ability to connect to God was shattered, and she attempted suicide. Tabitha lived in her bedroom for a year after the abuse. She has no memory of her two oldest children's weddings, which took place during this time.

Although Tabitha has seen a psychiatrist, several psychologists, and a social worker, she has not been able to find a helpful therapist. She left the church for several years, but recently returned. She has found supportive clergy within her denomination, yet she still struggles with feeling comfortable in church. It has been eleven years since the assaultive relationship ended.

Sarah

Sarah began attending church with her husband. She was eager to serve God and participated in many areas of church life. Her pastor, who was much older than she was, used Bible study as a way of manipulating Sarah into a sexual relationship with him. During the abuse, Sarah was depressed and suicidal, and she cut herself. After the abuse ended, she stopped going to church and felt spiritually devastated.

A pastor in a neighboring town was supportive and encouraged Sarah and her husband in their healing. Eventually, Sarah felt she was healed by God. She enrolled in a biblical counseling course, found this training helpful, and began an advocacy group for women who have been sexually abused by members of the clergy.

Today, Sarah is active in her denomination and in supporting laborers. Her denomination supports her advocacy work. It has been ten years since her assault.

Jessica

Jessica had always been active in her denomination. She had recently moved to a new community and was looking for a church of her denomination to join. She found a church she liked and sought out the female minister for counseling because she was struggling with her sexual orientation. In the course of counseling, the minister sexually assaulted her. Jessica left shocked, thinking, "What just happened to me is what is happening in the Catholic church."

Four years later, Jessica went to the denominational leadership to report the assault. The leaders were initially horrified and seemed inclined to launch a major response. But then the matter was taken behind closed doors, Jessica was shut out of the case, and nothing was ever done. Jessica was never told why nothing was done; however, she did hear comments about it being her word against the minister's word. She knows that the denomination spoke to members of the congregation where the abuse occurred, but the members they spoke with were supporters of the minister and had been identified *by the minister* as good people for them to speak to after the case was filed. The denominational leaders also brought up the fact that Jessica had not joined the congregation at the time she was assaulted. Jessica believes they thought this was relevant to the case because her lack of official membership in the congregation implied that her connection to the church was loose, although she had been attending and giving money to the church. The minister left the congregation prior to Jessica filing her complaint, and currently continues serving as a member of the clergy. The church's lack of response to Jessica's complaint and its failure to even issue an apology further traumatized her.

Today, Jessica attends church only when she is out of state and is able to visit two congregations in her denomination which she knows to be safe. Yet, she cringes if the minister mentions justice in the sermon because she has found no justice for herself in her denomination. She wonders if the denomination's failure to act was because she was assaulted by a clergywoman instead of a clergyman. Jessica was assaulted just over ten years ago.

Janet

Janet was born to a Jewish mother but was raised Christian. As an adult, Janet wanted to raise her child in the faith of her ancestors, so she turned to Judaism. She was eager to learn about it and became involved in many of the activities at the Reform Jewish temple. She eventually sought out her rabbi for counseling. The rabbi was friendly with all the women in the congregation. While counseling Janet, the rabbi attempted to persuade her to have "an affair" with him while he perpetrated sexual boundary violations against her behind the closed doors of his office. During that time, he also touched her inappropriately and kissed her before and after services in front of her young daughter and other congregants. When he learned she had told a friend at temple what he had done, he physically assaulted Janet. She eventually left the temple and sought out an Orthodox synagogue to attend. She chose to go to an Orthodox place of worship rather than a Reform one because Orthodox rabbis are not allowed to touch female congregants, so she felt safer there.

Janet later learned that the rabbi who had assaulted her had been sued earlier for sexual harassment of another female congregant. Janet then went to her Reform denomination and reported the rabbi for sexual misconduct. She also reported the sexual misconduct and assault to the Jewish press, naming the offending rabbi. After Janet went public with her story, most members of the Jewish community shunned her, and she went into hiding for a long time. The rabbi resigned from the temple where he had assaulted Janet and ultimately received a "slap on the wrist" by the Reform denomination, which had allowed him to continue in his role as rabbi and thereby continue to target female congregants. Janet was eventually told by a prominent member of her former temple that the rabbi apparently had a sexual relationship with a female congregant while her own case was being investigated by the Reform denomination. The rabbi wound up marrying this congregant, who is his third wife.

Janet stopped going to worship for a time and became skeptical of her tradition. Eventually, she was befriended by a Reform rabbi who was a rabbinic sexual misconduct prevention advocate. Today she has returned to a Reform temple and supports laborers in their healing. Unfortunately, her daughter will have nothing to do with the Jewish community or the Jewish faith due to what was done to her mother. Janet was assaulted nine years ago.

Jane

Jane joined the church because she learned others in her Al-Anon group had found supportive people in their congregations. Immediately, she became active in many programs and the priest began grooming her for sexual assault. When the priest moved to a new congregation in another state, Jane and a few others from the congregation later moved across state lines and joined the priest's new congregation. The priest Jane had followed sexually assaulted her, and she eventually became aware that another woman in the congregation was in a similar relationship with the priest. When Jane came forward with her story, the abusive clergyperson transferred his ordination to a splinter denomination.

The hierarchies in both his former denomination and the splinter denomination were unable to help Jane. Her denomination said that since he was no longer ordained in that denomination, they could not do anything. The splinter denomination claimed that because the assault had happened in his previous denomination, they did not have jurisdiction to act.

In the end, Jane was blamed by the congregation for the abuse, left the church, and has not returned. She became depressed and had difficulty functioning at work. Although she is a master's-level social worker, Jane did not recognize the relationship as a boundary violation until sometime after it ended. Jane was assaulted six years ago.

Juliana

Juliana was an ordained minister serving overseas, working with human-trafficking victims, when she was sexually assaulted by her superior. While he was visiting her from the United States, he began grooming her by sharing with Juliana personal information about his sexual relationship with his wife. Juliana said that when he started discussing this, she had feelings of fear but downplayed them and chose to offer him counsel. From his blurring of these boundaries, the abuse progressed. After her assault, Juliana's life began to unravel, though she still had a strong spiritual practice. She says, "After spending days in prayer, literally on my knees calling out to God, I felt like God directed me to come forward and tell my supervisors what had happened to me."

Her supervisors said they were not surprised to hear what she told them about this denominational leader. This angered Juliana and she felt betrayed. They asked her what she wanted in return. She asked them to pay for counseling for her in the States, and she asked that the denomination enact policies addressing clergy sexual misconduct. Additionally, she asked denominational leaders to seek out other potential victims. After several months and a promise by the denomination to make these changes, Juliana resigned and signed a silencing agreement with her denomination. She believed that they would fulfill their promises and that this agreement would protect her potential for future employment as an ordained minister. But she was wrong. The denomination never fulfilled their promise to make changes in their policies about clergy sexual misconduct and never looked for other victims. Juliana fell into a depression and was unable to hold a steady job. Her therapist did not recognize what had happened to her as abuse, so was unhelpful.

Recently, Juliana decided to break the silencing agreement and spoke with several supportive people from her former denomination. Their recognition of her experience as abuse enabled her to finally begin the healing process. Toward the end of my writing this book, Juliana contacted me and shared that she has since taken a job as a hospital chaplain. Juliana was assaulted five years and six months ago.

Lindsay

Lindsay had attended her church since childhood. The abusive pastor had been her youth pastor and had begun grooming her when she was twelve years old, though she was not raped until age twenty. Looking back, she now realizes that when the pastor led Bible study, he would subtly twist Scripture in a manipulative way. Women were also perceived as second-class citizens in this congregation. In addition to Lindsay, the pastor sexually assaulted other women and teenage girls of the congregation.

Charges were filed against the pastor, and Lindsay was asked to meet with the police. Although she initially did not want to do so, she eventually decided to take part in the trial, which involved six women. In response to the trial, many people left the church. Lindsay feels that after the pastor was charged, she was able to have a direct relationship with God for the first time.

Although she has had some support from people in the church, Lindsay feels that after the trial ended, people faded away at a time when she still needed their support. Today, Lindsay is involved with a new church and with SNAP. She is passionate about helping others, specifically human-trafficking victims. Her assaultive relationship ended three years ago.

Angela

Angela had been in counseling with her pastor when he hired her to be his secretary. Once she began working for him, he wanted to have counseling sessions during the work day. She did not want to mix work with her counseling, but eventually, she consented because he was so persistent. One day in his office while she was crying, he kissed her. She became upset, and he told her it was like a brother and sister kissing. She was confused and the grooming progressed. She did not know how to tell her husband what had happened and went through a period of self-hate while continuing to be groomed. Today, her husband knows about the kiss and her subsequent assault. He is a big support to her.

Angela and her family began to attend a new church, which connected her with a counselor. However, the abusive pastor found out what church they were attending and contacted her new pastor to develop a working relationship with him and that church. Angela and her family decided to leave their new church because, although their new pastor knew of her accusations, as well as another woman's accusations, against the abusive pastor, he still formed a working relationship with the offender and allowed him to become involved with his church. Angela began the process of filing a lawsuit against the congregation where the assault had occurred. However, the collusion she faced created great amounts of anxiety and she has currently postponed the lawsuit. Her assault happened three years ago.

Yasmine

Yasmine lives in the Middle East, was raised Muslim, and is married to a Muslim relative. She lived her life for God but had grown to believe Islam was not a religion of love and felt a lot of fear in it. She became attracted to the message of love in Christianity and was in the process of converting to Christianity at the time of her assault. In Yasmine's culture, when one spouse converts to a different religion, the couple is considered divorced, so Yasmine considered herself divorced from her husband. The priest who assaulted Yasmine told her of his "love" for her and said that after he was ordained, they would be married. She was in love with the priest, and they became involved. He wore a promise ring she had given him to his ordination. Once he was ordained, however, he told her there was a "slight problem"—that Catholic priests were not allowed to marry—but he said he was sure that would change in the future.

Living in a Muslim country, Yasmine had not known that Catholic priests could not marry and had trusted what she was being told by the offender. Eventually, she realized the priest was lying to her, and she told another priest what had happened. The priest she confided in arranged for her to go to the Vatican with her complaint. At the Vatican, she met some high officials in the Roman Catholic Church, who told her that what had happened to her was a normal thing. Then, the priest to whom she had confided the assault and with whom she had traveled to the Vatican tried to seduce her in her hotel room.

When Yasmine arrived back home, she was very isolated. In the Middle East, there is something called "woman's honor," which consists of women "swallowing" anything that happens to them because they do not want to be exposed and dishonor their family and their people. Although other women have been abused by priests in the Middle East, they have been unwilling to open up to Yasmine because of the shame that doing so would bring to them and their families. Yasmine mentioned that she knew one woman who admitted that priests and bishops abuse women, but the woman would not admit that she herself had been abused.

In the Middle East, husbands who believe their wives are "cheating" on them might kill them, along with the priest, so women keep their mouths shut, kill themselves to save face and clean their honor, or live the rest of their lives in agony and complete silence. The priests in the Middle East are well aware that this is the case, and this enables them to behave however they desire in regard to the women in their congregations. The priest's only fear is that someone other than the woman will tell a family member what is happening.

The abusive priest wrote Yasmine and threatened to tell her family and her husband what she had done. The priest was astounded when Yasmine told him that she didn't care because her husband and family already knew. In the Middle East, it is almost impossible for a woman to stay alive after converting, much less after an abusive sexual relationship. Yasmine's aunt was able to placate her angry male relatives. Yasmine said that once the priest knew that her husband and family were aware of the situation and that his threats were not going to work, she began receiving death threats from members of the priest's church.

Yasmine was eventually hospitalized for suicidal ideation. While in the hospital, she took care not to tell any of the doctors or nurses about her situation because she knew what they, with their traditional Middle Eastern mentality, could do to her. When she eventually confided in American doctors, both Christian and Muslim, they were unable or unwilling to help her. The only support the American doctors gave her was in the form of psychotropic medication.

Christians who know about Yasmine's situation have warned her that she could destroy an already persecuted church if she talks publicly about the abuse. Muslims who know tell her this is what she gets for converting.

Yasmine's husband is being patient with her because he believes that if he can forgive her and get her to convert back to Islam, he will be in a very good position with God. Yasmine is not interested in converting back to Islam, but she questions whether the God of Islam and the God of Christianity are only for men and are against women. She especially wonders this because the abusive priest has been promoted to be the director of a university, as well as serving two Catholic churches. He has also been interviewed by the international media, including *The New York Times* and *The Washington Post.*

Yasmine still struggles to believe she was victimized. She thinks that because she was an adult, she should have known better. She also thought what she was doing was for Jesus and she wanted to be a martyr.

Yasmine finds support and help in hearing the stories of Western women and learning more about clergy sexual abuse and assault through written materials. Yasmine's assault happened one and a half years ago.

Conclusion

All the women were virgins in their spiritual and faith journeys, and each was involved in and identified closely with her faith community. Regardless of whether the assault took the form of rape or a "love" relationship, the clergyperson was able to blur the boundaries and gain access to the virgin's soul, creating in her a soul wound. In the next two chapters, the laborers tell their stories in their own words.

Chapter 5

Life-Giving Waters: A Script in Three Acts

As I analyzed the transcribed interviews of the eighteen laborers, I realized the many commonalities and themes among them. Recognizing also the laborers' need and desire to share their experiences with others, I decided to present their stories in the spirit of a community by writing a script in which the laborers are members of a support group specifically for women who have been assaulted by a clergyperson. The script is designed around topics which would be important to address in such a group.

I have written this chapter as a three-act play because the laborers' words carry more power than any summary of their stories ever could. The script is written in *vox participare*,[46] meaning the lines come directly from the participants' voices via the interview transcripts.

Act I addresses the harmful stories that others have told about the laborers and the pain the laborers bear. This act can be viewed as complications to labor. Act II tells of things that have been important and helpful in labor. This act represents the birthing process. Act III is the story of rebirth. Although

---

[46] Monica Prendergast, "The Phenomena of Poetry in Research," in *Poetic Inquiry: Vibrant Voices in the Social Sciences*, ed. Monica Prendergast, Carl Leggo, and Pauline Sameshima (Rotterdam: Sense Publishers, 2009), xxii.

not all the laborers felt they had been reborn, elements of rebirth were present in all the women.

Some of the material I chose to include might make some readers uncomfortable by challenging notions of God and the church. I believe it was necessary to include this information not only because it portrays an accurate picture of the experience of many laborers, but also because it is important for family, friends, and professionals working with laborers to do their own self-reflection around any internal issues a laborer's faith crisis may create in them. Such faith crises are normal.

I have used regular font for the laborers' and narrator's words, *italics for setting the scene and cueing the actors,* [brackets] when a word has been added to clarify meaning for the reader, and **bold to highlight whose voice is being shared, as well as for act and scene changes.**

Act 1 – Complications to Labor: The Stories Laborers Are Told

Narrator: *(Stage left.)* This play demonstrates the process of rebirth after clergy sexual assault. Rebirth is not linear. It occurs on many levels, including the physical, economic, social, mental, sexual, emotional, psychological, and spiritual. Along the path to rebirth, a laborer's emotions are often triggered by events in her life that pull her back to the assault and the collusion which followed. Part of rebirth is learning how to minimize such triggers.

Act I tells of the complications that not only hindered laborers' rebirth after clergy sexual assault but added further injury to their soul wounds. As you listen carefully to the narratives in Act I, you will hear the damaging effects that collusion has on laborers. The stories and the gossip about laborers contain untruths that have been imposed on them and which they tend to internalize. Such untruths often lead to depression, post-traumatic stress disorder (PTSD), self-harm such as cutting, suicidal ideation, and other symptoms of abuse.

Scene 1: Collusion.

(Curtain opens. Seventeen women, ranging in age from the mid-twenties to the late seventies, are gathered in a semi-circle. All wear a scarlet A on their chest[47] *and stand looking at the floor, fidgeting and shifting their body weight uncomfortably until the first woman speaks. Then they slowly begin to engage in the conversation and make eye contact with one another.)*

Narrator: In sixteen instances, the laborers' assault was reported to the congregation or denomination. Although sixteen cases were reported, seventeen laborers experienced some degree of collusion by their church. *(Exits.)*

Laurie: Someone more wise than I said the church is the only Army that shoots its wounded. That's a great phrase. I was wounded but it was the leader of our particular Army that shot me, and all his little soldiers rallied around him.

Jessica: The most damage that was done to me was really around the complaint process and filing the complaint with the

---

[47] In Nathaniel Hawthorne's *The Scarlet Letter,* the heroine Hester Prynne, who is also a laborer, is convicted of adultery and forced to wear a scarlet A on her dress for the rest of her life as punishment for her "sin."

denomination. I think before that, I had this thought in my head that, "If they only knew, they would be horrified." But when they knew, they weren't horrified, and all of that was gone. It is hard for me to see how people could look at my case, as I told it to them, and not be [so] utterly outraged and upset by it that they would do something with that minister in question to show that this is not acceptable. And I think there is the part of me that lost hope, lost faith—all of that—thinking, "How can this be okay? How can they think that this is okay behavior?" It's either that or they don't believe me and I don't know which is worse.

Nancy: When I told the interim pastor what had happened because I was literally going crazy, his first sentence to me was, "Oh, my God! Poor Joe!" Joe is the minister who abused me. That ought to tell you how the whole thing went. I was so devastated with that one sentence. I will never forget that, ever. Ever!

Valerie: [A priest who is a family friend] came to our family reunion, and afterwards he asked me how I was doing and was I still involved in my church career. And I said, "No, but I am involved in SNAP," and I was going to go on and talk to him all about this [rape]. And immediately he said, "Oh, I hate those people. They have ruined so many of our priests' lives. They were accused of child abuse, child sexual abuse, just one time and now their priesthood is ruined." I said, "I can't believe you." He's the kind of priest that I was telling people I was going to see him again after so many years and I was looking forward to it. I would also say that if the church had about five thousand like him, it would be a whole different church. So I was sadly disappointed, and that just ruined any attempt I would have made to talk to him seriously about the subject.

Jane: I really just tried to talk to the bishop. I didn't really plan on giving a deposition. I just wanted to talk to him and say, "This happened to me and just listen to me." And he wouldn't even call me back on the phone, and so when I realized how much collusion there was and covering up, I just became disenchanted.

Susan: As soon as the perpetrator admitted he was guilty and left the [clergy] roster, all support [for me] from the synod and the bishop ended, and I was trying to seek counseling and I did get to go on a retreat for victims of clergy sexual abuse, and I remember at the time, the bishop said, "Okay, we'll pay for this retreat, but don't ask for anything because you're not getting it." Now, the perpetrator was offered all the counseling he wanted, which he didn't take. So I didn't feel very good about it.

Amy: I had been a survivor of early childhood sexual abuse. I think they felt they weren't responsible for this act that had happened. And somehow that kind of meant I had other issues that caused me to be in this situation. They didn't feel that they were financially obligated to take care of me because of what had happened with the pastor. And I was really angry about that because, like I said, the minister resigned and he got a full severance package. He was able to get all the benefits that go along with being a resigned minister and I was left with the need for counseling for more than [the] three months [I received].

Laurie: The bishop came from the synod where it happened and brought all of his best men, and I sat on one side of the table and all of these men sat on the other side of the table, and it was horrendous. It sounds odd when I say it, but I have not changed my mind since then; when someone comes to me and says, "Should I report this?" I say, "No, not to the church. Absolutely, report it as criminal or something else, but I would never recommend reporting it to the church." What they do to you, what they did to me, was dreadful. Oh my word, I'm five-foot-two, blonde-haired, blue-eyed, and I was sitting in this stale room and these men in their collars were on the other side of the table and they were just hurling questions at me like, "Did you wear a bra?" and "What kind of shorts did you have on?"

Yasmine: And sometimes [the priests] would say, "This is the devil's doing. It's not the priest who did this. And the devil is closer to woman than man, and he uses you as a bait to lure him. There are other priests who are doing the same thing. Everybody makes mistakes and you know you're just a woman. You're a normal woman. There are children who get raped. God was just testing [the priests] and he was rewarding them for their good work with some good women, and now [they] have to go back to the path of God."

Willow: I would not have been as self-destructive as I ultimately was had somebody in the church reached out, somebody in the goddamn cluster. You know, no other Lutheran church in this area reached out, and let me tell you, there's a bunch of them.

Juliana: It was the church that cut me off. The church that made the choice to say, "You will be silenced" and "What happened to you is not valid." And because of their actions, it's taken me a while to come to this conclusion, but I really believe that the abuse itself for me was not what ruined my relationship with God *(laughs)* and changed my faith. It was the church's response.

Sarah: No one ever was told the truth. It was just kept pretty quiet.

Yasmine: It's like a mafia. They all support each other.

(Lights dim.)

Scene 2: Blame.

(One more laborer joins the group, bringing the total to eighteen. All still wear an A on their chest. They are seated now.)

Yasmine: In the Middle East, when a woman is in a relationship, no matter what, she's always the wrong one, especially when it is a holy man. She is the devil. She's the wicked woman.

Amy: And my best friend in the church, I told her everything, and she said, "Well, you know I'm really sorry, but he called and disguised his voice and he told everybody who you were, and I'm sorry, but I'm gonna stick with him."

Willow: Nobody cared. Nobody wanted anything to do with this scarlet woman who had the audacity to have sex with the pastor. Because the bottom line is, they don't blame him; they blame me.

Amy: [The wife of the president of the church council] asked me a very curt question. She asked me if I was on medication and I told her I was, and she said what I thought was a very disgusting response, which was, "Well, that's good. That should completely knock your sex drive out." And then she got up and walked over to my husband and said, "I am so sorry for what happened to you."

Willow: People do not want to believe that the pastor who married them, the pastor who baptized their children, and the pastor who buried their parents is a sex offender. And they will do anything and everything to avoid looking at that possibility. It is easier to blame the women.

Yasmine: But the people, oh my God, the judgment. I mean, when they support you, half of your problem is solved, but when all [the people are] against you, making you feel like you're the wrong one and he's the right one— He has the Holy Spirit. He's God's messenger. No matter what he does. When he gets ordained, he gets the Spirit and he will always be a priest no matter what happens.

Tabitha: No place seemed safe. I was afraid of running into somebody from the church. And I can remember one time my husband said, "Let's go to the grocery store. Come with me." So I go for a ride to the grocery store, and my eyes just kept darting around. I was afraid somebody from the church was going to be there. I was a basket case. I was a mess.

Janet: I went out in public, but I was in hiding from the Jewish community.

Yasmine: I got threatening messages. I got death threats from people who pretended to be Al Qaeda, but then I traced the address and I saw it was from the same Christian denomination where he is from, from the same people, the same city, the same place.

Angela: They have written letters to the congregation. They have said that I have mental issues. And I'm thinking, "Are you serious?"

Yasmine: They make it a very normal thing, and if you're destroyed, that's your problem. That means you have a psychological problem. Go to a shrink. It makes me feel so bad.

(Lights dim.)

Scene 3: Career.

(Nine laborers remain seated on stage. Four wear clerical blouses, but the collar is missing from two of them and tattered in the case of the other two. A hymnal lies at the feet of a fifth laborer. On the floor next to the sixth laborer lies a high school religious curriculum from the early 1980s. The seventh woman has a crumpled church planner at her feet. The last two are tired and dazed. All appear disheveled, and they all wear the scarlet A on their chest.)

Sharon: He stole that path that I had followed. My life had changed radically from the way I had prepared my life to be in terms of the way I was raised, my enthusiasm for the church, the career that I had prepared myself for, the jobs I had started out doing, and doing well, with a lot of enthusiasm. As a result of Joe manipulating me to have a sexual relationship with him, not only did I feel like I was damaged goods for another Catholic man—and now, incidentally, I know that that's not true, but at the time I didn't—but I became a person who was not the person that I was expecting to be. And my life, which had revolved around the church, no longer revolved around the church, and my career turned out to be something that I had not prepared myself to be.

Juliana: I was an incredible minister. I was really good at what I did. I was well known. I was sought after as a speaker for conferences and retreats and all that kind of stuff. I mean, there I was, and I don't have that anymore. You know, the potential for affecting people's lives was stolen, too, and that's just huge.

Nancy: Sometimes I still think about going to seminary, and then I think, "Naw, I couldn't do it. The whole church community thing."

Laurie: I was on my way. I was a youth pastor at this church, and he was the senior pastor and he was mentoring me, and we had even been down to Luther Northwestern Seminary. I mean, that was the plan. I always knew what I was meant to be since I was a little girl, and my dad always used to tell people that I'd be the first Lutheran pope *(laughing)*. And then when Joe decided he wanted to have sex with me, that was the end of that.

Susan: At the time he was being reinstated was the same time the ELCA was putting me through hell to grant me disability. So, while I was fighting the ELCA with one appeal after another to stay on the clergy roster, he was put back on. Basically without question.

Juliana: You didn't just rape this person. You didn't just commit inappropriate behavior with this person. You took everything from her, and it has eternal consequences.

(Lights dim.)

Scene 4: Faith Crisis.

(Fifteen laborers now sit in the group. All wear a scarlet A on their chest.)

Sarah: It was so difficult at first to learn to trust God again and to allow his Word to be a comfort to me, not a trigger.

Valerie: I feel a sense of emptiness sometimes because I don't have anything in my life at this time that encourages me as far as spirituality is concerned.

Jane: I felt like the church had betrayed me. And somehow that translated into God had betrayed me, too.

Juliana: Going to church was almost impossible.

Susan: The church is the one that defines who's acceptable and who's loved.

Tabitha: Where there's real faith, it just destroys it and makes it hard to see. I think it's just the devil's work. It's gotta be.

Susan: So much of my spirituality throughout my whole life was tied to the church. My family always went to church, my dad was an elder, my mom was an organist and a Sunday School teacher. So much of my identity as a believer and a follower of Jesus was tied up in the institution of the church, and then my identity as a pastor, and I have so soured on the church. I feel like my spirituality has been stolen by them as well. That there's nothing left. I don't have anything left.

Jessica: It made me lose hope in humanity. The word "justice" in any sermon was enough to [make me] suddenly fly out of the pew 'cause I was just feeling like there is no justice and how could you be talking about believing in justice and working for justice when you know everything that happened with me clearly was unjust in how I was treated, particularly in the denomination. That demonstrated to me that justice is something that people just like to talk about but that it is not for real, at least among the people I interacted with.

Tabitha: I can't trust. It's all phony and I guess I was just stupid even to believe such a stupid thing. I had a picture back before the abuse and during the abuse. It was a picture of Jesus holding this lamb and I had it on my nightstand. It was a place where I would do my Bible study. I remember one day I was looking up at that [picture] and I threw it out the window. I was angry. I thought, "I'm not that little sheep. How could somebody tell me I was? I'm not!"

Susan: That God had such great love for all that he sent his Son to die. I really struggle with crucifixion and have not had resurrection. I don't really understand the concept of crucifixion and resurrection. That doesn't really mean anything to me. I don't get it. That's why I have a hard time with Jesus as the Son of God or Jesus as divine. I know a lot about crucifixion *(laughs).* I don't know anything about resurrection from my own personal experience with the church.

Jane: If your soul can be nauseated, then mine was.

Janet: I had such joy in my religion and it's just, it's not really there anymore. I questioned whether there was even a G-d.

Amy: I had to be quiet to God for a while.

Angela: It's just so hard for me. They really just took my spirit. I started not believing that there was a God. What kind of God would allow people to suffer like that? All my life, suffering. Lord, why do I have to suffer? Why do I have to continue to suffer?

Yasmine: And sometimes I feel suicidal because my life was for God and later on there is no meaning to my life. Is this against God? Does God hate me that much? Does he hate women? Is he standing up with men? Okay, if he hates women, then why did he create us? He might as well not have created us, and it made me [feel] more hated. It made me [feel] unloved. It made me feel that there is no religion, no path, no way to God. So, who is God? Where is God? How can I reach him? If there is no religion, how can I talk to him? Why doesn't he talk to me? Where is he? I'm all alone. And I'd start crying.

(Lights dim.)

Scene 5: Unhelpful Counseling and Advice.

(All the laborers are on stage in the semi-circle. They still wear the letter A on their chests.)

Narrator: *(Stage left.)* Although professional clinicians are not paid to give advice, unhelpful counseling and advice have been grouped together because one of the many things unhelpful clinicians did was to offer advice. The laborers now share some of what they found to be unhelpful. *(Exits.)*

Amy: I have a minister friend who says, "Amy, you really need to go to church. You need it more than you know." And I'm like, "What is that supposed to mean?" How do you get through all that?

Rosa: That's a big turn-off when people start trying to preach to me to do the Catholic thing. Don't start shoving that down my throat like that's the way, the end-all and be-all, 'cause it isn't. And the Bible, same thing. I'm not going to live my life according to the Bible. And I resent [it] when people try to push that on me, too. That's where I'm going to find my salvation? No, I don't agree. God's bigger than religion. That's my point, and I know I'm still struggling but I don't feel like my answer is because I haven't been going to church or reading the Bible, that that's why I'm stuck the way I am. No! I don't think that.

Yasmine: The doctor would tell me, "It's confusing how to deal with patients like you because I don't want to impose a religion on you, but the only way to solve your problem is for you to find a religion and I just can't do this to you and you can't get this thing solved without this." And I just thought, this isn't going to help because you just can't tell me, "Just stop thinking about it. Go find a hobby. Go find friends and forget about it." That's not going to work. And he thought that medication would be the only way. So I'm on the medication.

Tabitha: I've had a lot of counseling: a psychiatrist, a couple of psychologists, a social worker. I can't say that any of the counseling was very helpful, though. You know, they don't even understand it too much. Well, I guess it kept me alive, and day-to-day things. Cognitive behavioral therapy. Just pretty much helping me exist. There was some value in it. But it didn't help me spiritually any, I don't think. I really never talked to anybody about the spiritual part of it at all. People just didn't get it. I even had one woman ask me, "Is this wrong for him to do what he did?" and I'm like, "Oh my gosh!"

Valerie: [The therapist] said, "It had to be romantic." And I said, "How can a rape be romantic?"

Jessica: [A minister I told] encouraged me to file the complaint initially with the denomination. And then there came a time when the feeling I got from her was that I should be over it and that I should have healed and that I [had] passed the information on to the denomination and I should just be able to walk away now and kind of get over it. And I wasn't over it, and so that's largely what led me to leaving the church—feeling like I wasn't getting support from her and feeling worse and worse that I wasn't healed yet on whatever her timetable was.

Valerie: I wanted to know how you can believe in a Higher Power that AA talks about all the time. And [the priest] said he couldn't help me with it *(laughs).* I did not tell him anything about the abuse but he just said he couldn't help me with [how to believe in a Higher Power], and I thought, "Good Lord, what the heck does he think he's in this business for?"

Yasmine: One therapist told me, "What exactly do you want to do, go against the whole church? Are you crazy? Of course you can't do this. You want justice? You'll never get justice. There are [people even worse off] than you. Just leave this whole thing."

Jessica: [The therapist specializing in clergy sexual abuse] wanted to lump me in with everyone else who experienced [clergy sexual] abuse rather than being able to listen individually to what my experience was. I mean, I think there's something helpful in knowing that you are not alone and that other people have the same feelings, [but] I think it's not helpful when you feel somewhat like you're being dismissed: "Oh, you're just another person who went through clergy abuse; therefore, you feel X, Y, and Z."

Rosa: I can't see [my therapist] right now. She doesn't go through insurance, and I'm very badly missing having therapy and it's not fair the church won't pay for it. I have to pay for it myself and I can't afford it right now.

(Lights dim.)

Scene 6: Grief.

(All eighteen laborers are seated on stage. All wear black with a scarlet A on their chest.)

Narrator: *(Stage left.)* Although grief was not discussed in every interview, all laborers exhibited elements of grief. *(Exits.)*

Jane: I just felt like my life was anguish all the time. And I had a hard time for at least a year thinking about anything else. It was as if you had lost your child. Every moment of every day was colored by the loss. I couldn't see except through the lens of loss, of all the losses that were involved. It hurt on a lot of levels. And I barely got through it. At the time, I felt like I was in pieces all over the place. It felt like putting it together again, getting myself together again, was like picking up one broken piece at a time. Like a vase that's beautiful, shattered in a million pieces, and all you can do is, maybe one time a week, you can put one piece back, and I don't think it's finished. I think I keep finding pieces *(laughs)*. And I work on them one at a time. So when people say "it's shattering," that resonates with me. Nothing in my life that I took for granted was quite there anymore. I had to look at it and see where it fit again.

Angela: I need to move beyond them, but it's just sort of hard when I grew up in that circle so long.

Laurie: I was a mess. I lost my job, and then I lost my other job. The two jobs: the church and the resort. I lost my home. I lost my church family. I lost my friends. I lost my identity. I lost my identity. *(Silence.)* I lost my identity. That's what I was created to be doing. And I'm a mess. When you think of a mess in the kitchen—I don't cook, my husband does all of the cooking, so when I cook, it's a mess—and that's how everything was. My life was poured out. There were chunks of tomato over there, and chunks of pineapple over there, and red sauce and white sauce. I was a mess. And everything had melted down. Someone had stabbed my heart, and the ELCA guys were stabbing me in the back. I was a mess. I was bleeding everywhere, and nobody could fix it. And nobody has been able to fix it. *(Silence.)* I mean, they've helped me move on but my life was destroyed, and when they talk about victimization, I'm the victim! I mean, for the pastor to still be pastoring! I mean, if I let that, every day that could destroy me! *(Silence.)* Yeah, I was a mess. I mean, I didn't know who I was. The only part of me that I knew who I was still followed Jesus Christ. That does not change. Everything else changed. I mean, I changed the color of my hair. I got fat. My job changed. My location changed. I changed my car. I mean, everything changed. I believe we are all created with certain gifts and talents, and when you are doing what God created you to do, you are at peace and the world is being changed for the better. And when you're not, you're a mess. That's what I think *(laughing)*. And I'm still a mess because when that is taken from you, to get back there, oh man. I think my [call to ministry] was given to me. It was a gift and I was there. So, you see the part of me that is still a mess. I just get crazy thinking about it. So I can portray to the world a plate of spaghetti and meatballs with really tidy red sauce on top, but the reality is the red sauce is EVERYWHERE and the meatballs are off the planet!

(Silence.)

Susan: I was a virgin when I was raped.

(Lights dim.)

Scene 7: Post-Traumatic Stress Disorder (PTSD) and Other Symptoms.

(All eighteen women are in the semi-circle. They are all bandaged. The scarlet A is still displayed on their chests.)

Jane: It's like getting back from the war. You can get help, you can have a good life again, but you may have certain symptoms that are a part of life. So for me, I do have flashbacks. I still have bad dreams. I have different capacity to fall asleep at night. So, dealing with the traumatic memories, I think that's part of your brain that's very hard to deal with because that's where you tuck those memories in. I've been damaged, so I feel like I'm a wounded healed person. You know what I mean? The post-traumatic stress is like that gift that keeps on giving. And I have to live with that. As if the experience had left me with no legs. I can heal but I still have no legs. I think that's how I see the post-traumatic stress and some of its symptoms. They have abated, but I have a feeling that they're going to be with me for a while, and I don't know how long, if it's forever? But that's the part that's changed my life.

Rosa: I never had the PTSD before the exploitation by the priest. All the years that I was working on the incest and my family dysfunction, never once was it suggested I take medication. Not until after the exploitation.

Susan: I was just falling apart. I was starting to have [visual] hallucinations and auditory [hallucinations].

Amy: I couldn't even function.

Tabitha: I don't remember a whole lot during those first couple of years. [If I went to church], it was just real, kinda, just sorta blackout in my head and freak-out, a little bit like a panic attack. I just would get the heart racing and the room spinning and I'd leave or cry. Cry a lot. I would cry a lot. It was just so dark and so depressing. I [eventually] stayed home. I didn't leave the house. It was just super-depression. It was horrible.

Dee: When I remembered the whole thing, it played in front of my eyes just like a fast-forward on a football game would play. And I thought, "NO! No, no, no, no!" And it played again and I thought, "Oh, oh!" but I thought, "Oh, ministers don't do that kind of thing!" It played the third time and I went, "Oooh, ooooooh, oooh, oh, oh, okay, I know. Now I know what really happened. I know what happened to me, but this is one thing I will go to my grave with. I will never tell anyone this terrible thing I have done." That's victim talk. Then I raged for about three days. I was by myself in that situation, and by the end of the third day I had it pretty much stuffed down, and I didn't remember again until I came back home a couple of months later.

Angela: The only thing I feel like right now is that I'm an outcast. And I've just been praying to God. My prayer to God now is, "Lord, I don't want to die in this shame."

Amy: Some days I'll go along and I'll be fine, and other days I'll go along and have extreme, profound sadness and I'll wonder what's going on with me and I just sort of sit with those feelings and I let them be what they are, and usually what happens is that it's a trigger or it's an anniversary time because, I think, trauma is stored in the body and I think our body remembers different things, and either some person will trigger me or a time period will trigger me, and so, you know, I just try to take care of myself.

Lindsay: I did go the medication route temporarily, and I think that definitely helped, especially going through the trial experience, and I had a lot of trouble with sleeping and stuff like that.

Amy: I want to believe that all the good things he said about me were true *(crying)*. If I hate him and I say that he was a bad person, then that would be saying that none of those things he was saying about myself were true. That is really difficult to know, whether they were true or lies. I think the difficult thing for any woman that is in this situation—at least that's been my experience—[is] so much anguish. It's a conflict of feelings. It's deep anguish.

Yasmine: I was trying to hurt myself and I was taken to the hospital and I stayed there for two weeks.

Tabitha: I was in the hospital after I had taken all those pills.

Amy: How do I forgive him?

(Silence as the lighting fades. Narrator enters.)

Narrator: *(Stage left.)* The mental and spiritual health of all eighteen laborers was affected. Symptoms of the assault and collusion are listed by the frequency in which they were reported: inability to perform spiritual practices; depression; post-traumatic stress disorder (PTSD); anxiety; suicidal ideation and/or attempts; loss of faith; grief; dissociation, no memory of the abuse, limited memory after the abuse; inability to function; anger at God, offending pastor, church, self; excessive drinking; and self-harm, such as cutting.

(Curtain closes.)

Act II – Labor and the Birthing Process: Stories that Heal

Narrator: *(Stage left.)* In Act II, what was helpful to laborers in the labor process is revealed. As you watch this act, listen for how reframing the laborers' stories positively and how supportive relationships shift the laborers' paradigm of shame to one of strength and possibility, offering them healing glimpses of hope and justice. *(Exits.)*

Scene 1: Justice.

(Curtain opens. In this scene, four laborers separate themselves out from the remaining fourteen. These are the four who experienced a sense of justice. The four are dressed nicely. The remaining fourteen wear casual clothes. The scarlet A's have permanently been removed from everyone's clothing.)

Lindsay: He got forty years in prison. I was very happy with the outcome and that's what I wanted. Through the prosecutor's office, they have a program called Victim Assistance, and they pay for your counseling, your medication, you know, different therapy pieces: if someone would have to be hospitalized, if they had damaged property or loss of work. There's a lot of different pieces that they will participate in. But I mean, they probably paid thousands of dollars for my therapy and different things I've had to do. That was a huge blessing.

Sarah: [A pastor] came and met with [my husband and me] and expressed his anger at what the abusive pastor had done. He was one of the first to call it abuse and tell us that it was wrong and it wasn't my fault. He was very accepting, compassionate, and caring toward both of us. He knew how badly we had been hurt and that we needed time to heal. He helped us through that very painful stage, as we were only able to sit through church and not be actively involved for a time.

Janet: This rabbi who has been my mentor for a long time—he's the one who really made me feel "Yes, I'm the victim. No, I didn't do anything wrong. No, I didn't ask for it. And yes, he believed me." And that was my first step toward healing, and he has been my touchstone all along to where, if I'm having problems or I need help with another [survivor], I call him and he's right there to help. So, he was probably the most important person that I was led to that helped me to heal.

Juliana: I decided I needed to tell [the pastor whose congregation supported my overseas mission work] what had happened. So, in April of [last] year, at the end of the month, I went to [see him] and told him. He believed me. He validated me. He said everything that I needed to hear that I didn't know I needed to hear. He cried. And I said, "This is the last step of the journey and I really don't care about what happens to the denomination, but I really felt that you ought to know what they've done. You know, you can just do with this story whatever you want, but it's yours and I hand it to you." He said, "Well, this is wrong, and I want to fight for you, and I want to confront the denomination for what they've done to you." He said, "You don't have to be a part of that unless you want to be and feel you have the energy to be, but it doesn't matter. I believe your story. This is wrong, and they need to be held accountable for that." So he started his own process of confronting the denomination, the top leaders of the denomination, about what had happened. And that process started immediately. He called people that evening after he spoke with me and started telling my story with my permission to other denominational leaders and to other influential pastors in the country. In doing that, he told me that day, "I want to be your pastor." And he said, "If you don't want me as a pastor because you don't even believe in God, that's okay. I will be your friend. I'm in this with you. And I care about you. And I'll be praying for you." His commitment to justice on my behalf against his denomination, an entire entity—him making that commitment that had the potential to affect his own career 'cause he was going up against the big dogs and he's a young man—his decision to do that made a big impact on me.

(Silence as the fourteen who have not experienced justice think about what they just heard. Eventually, Jane stands.)

Jane: My sense of justice is that we're here to make justice, not that God is going to do it.

Narrator: *(Stage left.)* Although a number of clergy were defrocked, the laborers did not feel this was enough to count as justice. This is because after disclosure was made to congregations, most laborers were blamed, shamed, and driven from their faith communities. Restorative justice demands that those who have been injured be fully restored to community. Justice is a basic tenet of Judaism, Christianity, Islam, and Unitarianism and it needs to be practiced as well as preached.

(Lights dim.)

Scene 2: Helpful Counseling.

(Sixteen laborers are now seated in a semi-circle. They are all dressed casually.)

Narrator: *(Stage left.)* Although two of the laborers were unable to find clinicians to help them, sixteen eventually found helpful ones. Helpful clinicians provided a safe space, and were validating, supportive, and protective. They understood PTSD, religious abuse, boundary violations, spiritual healing, and spirituality. They taught the laborers what clergy sexual assault was and stressed the laborers' innocence in the abusive relationship. All laborers stressed that learning the dynamics of the abusive relationship was an important factor in their rebirthing. *(Exits.)*

Laurie: [A pastor] said to me that it would not matter if the Rockettes danced naked—I love this line—if the Rockettes danced naked before this man, it's his responsibility to not do anything. It doesn't matter if you were cute. It doesn't matter if you dressed fashionably.

Juliana: My therapist says, "There's nothing wrong with you. You're not mentally ill. You were traumatized. You have PTSD."

Willow: I remember Sister Ann telling me, "You can be pissed off with God. God doesn't care. God is big enough, so tell God exactly what you think because God's shoulders are big enough to hear it." I can still hear her telling me that stuff and giving me that permission to be pissed at God, and in being pissed at God I found a different life.

Susan: I just felt like I really needed to have a real in-depth groping of what I call the muck of my soul. And that was really hard.

Amy: I was going to outpatient therapy at the hospital where I was admitted, and I remember sitting there making a list, and I was writing in a journal and I wrote, "I am going to make spaghetti today." It was like a major accomplishment to make a list of things, and it seemed like it was a foreign thing to do.

Narrator: *(Stage left.)* Some clinicians offered group therapy for women who were assaulted by members of the clergy or for sexual abuse survivors in general. Some laborers found psychoanalysis, such as Jungian dream work, helpful. Some found cognitive behavioral therapy beneficial, especially when used in conjunction with spiritual counseling. One found helpful a Christian counselor specializing in sexual abuse who prayed at the end of her sessions. Others appreciated therapists who also held seminary or religious degrees. Clinicians who recommended reading materials were appreciated. And one even advocated with the denomination on behalf of the laborer. One clinician had many characteristics similar to the abusive minister, and the transference issues that arose were healing to the laborer.

(Lights dim.)

Scene 3: Supportive Relationships.

(Sixteen women are in the group. Two are absent. All present are dressed casually.)

Narrator: *(Stage left.)* Laborers found support from family, friends, clergy, and clinicians. Especially helpful were retreats for laborers, support from other laborers, SNAP, internet websites, national advocates, online articles, chat rooms, and books. Some laborers found support in new churches and church groups and in others who had left the abusive congregation. One found support in a congregation that had removed an offending clergyperson and then had done healing work, as a congregation, around clergy sexual assault. Twelve-step programs such as Alcoholics Anonymous, Codependents Anonymous, Al-Anon, and Sexual and Love Addicts Anonymous were also supportive and provided laborers an avenue to reconstruct their spiritual beliefs. Let's listen in as their discussion focuses on support. *(Exits.)*

Laurie: Pastor Harry and Pastor Peter and Pastor Tim said, "The guy's a predator." That's what my personal support team said, and they wrote letters to the bishop and said, "This is wrong! How you've treated her is wrong!" And then they encouraged me every time it came into my mind to say, "Father, forgive them, for they know not what they do," as a way to let it go.

Nancy: He and his wife are both ministers there. And they immediately surrounded me in protection. So I left the Lutheran church and went to that church. And anything I wanted to do—lawsuits, no lawsuits, newspaper, no newspaper—they said, "We stand behind you 100 percent."

Amy: This man, a rabbi, said, "No, he didn't take your soul away from you." And he gave me some words, he described how horrific my experience was because I had told him in great detail everything, and he said, "What's really happened, Amy, is you have fallen awake to yourself." And I really like that idea, even though it didn't really make any sense to me at that time. He said I [had] completely unhinged from my life.

Jane: [A national advocate] gave me a lot of wise words and support, and a lot of repeating to me that "you are not 99 percent guilt-free or responsibility-free; you are 100 percent responsibility-free. This wasn't even 1 percent your responsibility." This helped me to see it as a social worker, that if the tables were turned and I had started doing any of the grooming things, that would be unethical and I would never even do that.

Amy: And I got home and went online and told some of these people who had been trying to help me what I had done, and they were cheering for me; they were like, "Yay! Yay! Good! This is good! You confronted him. You confronted the beast." It was a good thing.

Dee: They fully supported me. If it had not been for those women that surrounded me that evening, I don't know what I would have done. They didn't understand it, of course. Didn't have a clue. But they believed me. And they were my support from then on.

Nancy: They did a workshop based on [clergy sexual abuse], and that was very helpful and very healing to be in a room with people who had gone through the same thing.

Valerie: I joined that church for a while, and I was invited to come back for an occasion there, a Mass, and then we had some breakfast and conversation down in the auditorium below the church. Those people hadn't seen me in quite a while, and every single one of them came up and gave me a big hug. And that meant so much and it was like a family, a real community. And that has probably meant more to me than anything that has ever happened to me in my life.

Susan: The [head chaplain of the fleet] said, "I've received more unsolicited praise for you than any other chaplain in the whole fleet. I just assumed everything I heard about you was correct. I never asked you your side of the story." So he said, "Tell me what happened." So I told him, and he was just livid. He couldn't believe it. So he also became a strong support, and he still is today. But unfortunately, by standing up for me and another female chaplain, he was blackballed by the priests and by his diocese and by the Navy.

Amy: I call [my friend] and say, "Will you just listen to me cry for a minute?" And I'll just talk to her on the phone and tell her what is going on, and as soon as I cry and tell her what it is, she'll say, "Oh, I'm so sorry. That's so awful." And then I'll feel fine and I can go on.

Nancy: I'll never forget this either: A [female minister] apologized to me on behalf of the ELCA for the way I was treated and for the way that the congregation treated me.

(Lights dim; narrator enters stage left.)

Narrator: Two women were missing from this conversation. That is because they feel they have no supportive people in their lives. This is why it is vital that congregants learn about clergy sexual assault and that they reach out with compassion to laborers rather than further isolating and alienating them.

(Spotlight fades.)

Scene 4: Humor, Healing Distance, and Making Choices.

(All the participants are in the group now because they all can use a hearty laugh. They are seated in more relaxed postures than they have been in the past.)

Narrator: *(Stage left.)* Some of the laborers used humor as a way of coping with the betrayal and shunning they experienced. *(Exits.)*

Laurie: Well, the only joke I make about this whole thing is, with the check [from suing the church] I bought—and if this language offends you, I'm sorry; I don't say this as a practice—but I bought fuck-you earrings. I bought real pearls and real diamonds with that money, and that was my way of saying that to the ELCA. That always makes me smile.

Dee: I meet church members at funerals and I don't really do a lot in town, but when I do, it's always like, "Oh, haven't seen you in a long time. How are you?" And my reply is, "Never been better." *(laughing)* You know, if you want to live in your denial, go right ahead, but I don't spend a lot of time [there].

Laurie: Find whatever makes you laugh. Laugh. Belly-laugh. You must belly-laugh until you pee in your pants. Now, I only pee in my pants because I'm over fifty and probably menopausal, but you've got to belly-laugh. You've got to laugh it out. You find the person or the movie or whatever it is and you belly-laugh.

Narrator: *(Stage left.)* Many laborers mention the passage of time as lessening the pain of the assault. But not all the laborers agreed that time heals all wounds. Some mention their determination in sticking to the choice to heal, which required continually putting their decision into action. *(Exits.)*

Dee: It's about healing and coming back into alignment so that you can be fully present and have that calm and peace because we are our breath. Our breath is what our life is.

Janet: It's no magic pill. It really takes a long time and it's hard to do, but I think eventually it kind of sunk into my psyche that the longer I go to the good place, the further I get from the bad place.

Dee: Things come up; you have to learn not to react and you don't take it in and you don't let it bother you. When somebody brings up some little thing, I just let that go on by. That's their experience. That's their little thing. I do not need to react to this. I don't need to go there. I know what triggers that inside me, so I can quiet that inside and I don't need to go there. Don't need to go there at all. Just let it pass on by. Do you want to recover? Get the real revenge: recover. Or do you want to let the damn thing kill you? I'm not about to let the damn thing kill me *(laughing).*

(Curtain closes.)

Act III: Rebirth

Narrator: *(Stage left.)* In this act, laborers share accounts of their rebirth. Remember, rebirth does not mean returning to who they were before the abuse, but being transformed by the darkness into which they were thrust. For some of them, many years have passed since their assault. For others, it has only been a little more than a year.

Scene 1: Community.

(Curtain opens. All eighteen laborers are gathered in a group.)

Narrator: *(Stage left.)* Many laborers mention the desire to find a spiritual community. Some places where they have found community are friendships with other laborers, non-profit justice and advocacy groups, twelve-step groups, athletic groups, and welding class. And some no longer seek community. *(Exits.)*

Nancy: One thing that is very different about me since [the abuse]: I'd rather be by myself. I'm very wary about getting too close to people. I mean, I'm friendly to people and all that sort of thing, but I don't have groups of close friends. I just keep my distance.

Amy: The way I feel about it is that this twelve-step meeting has become my church.

Susan: This community I joined is one of incredible support and love. They have a statement of affirmation and it's our creed; it's love. I can't remember how it goes, but something about service to others and loving one another and that's basically it. No matter where you come in your faith journey, whether you believe in God or not. We have atheists who come there. Like one guy, he does our newsletter, and he's one of the most loving people I've ever met.

Juliana: This church is different somehow. Jesus is portrayed as sort of a radical community organizer that wanted folks to understand an inclusive God, a God who wanted to be a part of their daily lives, as opposed to the "normal" church who focuses on sin and redemption, and the brutality of the cross as a way to demonstrate God's love. There is an avoidance of any patriarchy in the sermons, in the music, in the readings. Even in the bulletin, they don't capitalize any words, not even "god" or "jesus." The language in the songs is modified or we simply sing another kind of song that you wouldn't find in a hymnal. The readings come from all religious traditions, even pagan, and include non-religious writings. The Bible is still read as a part of that, but read and interpreted in a way that is somehow comfortable for me for the first time in a long time. The community is one that includes and involves everyone: gays, lesbians, transgender, old, young, etc. Nobody seems to care who you are. Everybody appears to be broken in their own way, and they have chosen to be on the journey of life together. The focus on earth-based spirituality or "creation spirituality," as defined by Matthew Fox, connects me to where I had found solace in these last few years: in nature. The congruency of that, I think, also helps me not feel like I'm making a big jump backwards into some kind of religion that I had abandoned, but forwards into a belief that could somehow incorporate nature and indigenous beliefs with some of what I have known in the past.

(Lights dim.)

Scene 2: Trust.

(Although few laborers speak in this scene, all listen attentively.)

Narrator: *(Stage left.)* Rebirth does not necessarily mean returning to a semblance of how one used to be. Some things are lost, and rebirth means coming to a place of acceptance with the loss and incorporating it into one's identity. One of the ways in which most of the laborers changed was in their ability to trust. *(Exits.)*

Juliana: I think that trust is one of our basic needs as human beings, and trust for me was destroyed. It was destroyed individually with this person who did this to me. It was destroyed [systemically] within the church. It was destroyed in my family and their reaction to me. Trust was destroyed. And to trust anybody or anything or any God was impossible. I feel like a little girl who's been severely abused and looks at adults out of the sides of her eyes, kind of [like], "I don't know about you. I don't know if I can trust you. But for whatever reason you seem to be okay, so I'm going to take a huge risk and give you a chance." And only recently, in response to these three individuals [from my former denomination who acted on my

behalf] in the last couple of months, has there been any semblance of trust. A trust that somebody might actually be trustworthy other than my husband.
Janet: I used to trust people initially; now people have to earn my trust. So that changed 100 percent.

Sarah: I no longer extend automatic, blanket trust to anyone, not even a spiritual leader. Trust, like respect, must be earned, and only those who are truly trustworthy gain my trust. I have a healthier sense of trust now—not cynical, but not automatic.

Angela: Because, you know, I trust myself 100 percent, but I don't trust anybody else. Does that make sense? You know, I trust what *I'm* not going to do, but I don't trust *you*. I don't trust that Christian. I don't trust that Christian, that you're going to love me in a Godly manner. I'll trust you as far as I can see you now. That's the difference. But me, I trust.

(Lights dim.)

Scene 3: Meaning.

(The eighteen laborers are seated, listening attentively to those who speak.)

Narrator: *(Stage left.)* Recreating a sense of meaning in their lives is an important aspect of rebirth. The laborers share what gives them hope and their lives, meaning. *(Exits.)*

Lindsay: This isn't something that God wants to happen to you. His plan isn't that he wants this to happen. It isn't that he's out of control; it's just that he gives us free will. Every human being, whether they're a believer or not, has the freedom to choose. We all make bad decisions, wrong decisions, and people that are evil especially make decisions that are hurtful to other people, and because God gives us that freedom to choose, bad things happen. And that was primarily the way for me to be able to process it. That this wasn't the part of God's good plan or purpose for me. I think it is a situation that he can use in the future. I think sexual abuse and human trafficking aren't identical but there are a lot of similarities. So, I kind of feel like [working with human-trafficking victims is] my passion, and that's my calling, and that's going to be my ministry.

Juliana: It gives hope to me that if we were to teach survivors someday or churches someday that even if it's ten years since it's happened to somebody, if you reach out with trust, faith, and hope in that person and belief in that person and fight for their justice, you could help them recover even ten years later.

Yasmine: This [collusion] only makes me more determined to do something about it.

Amy: I can honestly tell you, a lot of men who come into those [twelve-step] meetings are ministers, and I know there are some sick ones who struggle and are trying to find recovery for themselves for the things that they've done that have been in a similar vein as my experience. So I've been able to speak to them in a way they needed to hear in order to understand the pain and the suffering that their behavior has caused the people they have been involved with in their life.

Valerie: When someone has been coming to [SNAP] meetings for a while and they finally get up the guts to tell their story, that's very rewarding. I've experienced several occasions like that. It becomes a joyful event.

Dee: I do an active ministry, whether it's with Al-Anon or any woman who comes across my path through email, and I've walked with some pretty trying cases, but I've walked with them. It's been wonderful.

Tabitha: One thing I think is always good is to try and keep somebody else from getting hurt. It is a good way to become spiritual again, I think, because God says nothing happens that he can't make good of, and I guess I believe that.

Jane: No matter how harsh truth is or how disillusioning, I'm the type of person that would rather know it. There's going to be times I'm going to be able to use what happened to me as a victim to help other people going through it, whether it's by reaching out one-on-one or being someone's mentor, or I'm going to write about it. I did write an article for a newspaper. I think that this is a way I'm called to help other people, raise consciousness about the issue. And I see that as a positive. There needs to be more things done channeling the energy into something that can make a difference, in whatever way, small or big, in terms of increasing awareness. That's why I tell people *(laughing)*. If it comes up in conversation I'm like, "Yeah, I was a victim of clergy sexual misconduct and abuse." And they're like, "Oh, okay." Some people just turn the other way and some are, like, "What do you mean?" and then I tell them. And they are, like, "But you were an adult." And I'm, like, "No." I'm walking around with my educator badge on all the time.

Janet: Rabbi [said], "We can't choose who G-d decides to [have] fight in the trenches against this problem because it is a war that we are fighting." And he said, "You've been chosen to be a foot soldier and to stand in that trench, in that fox hole, and so now it's up to you, it's up to you whether you're going to do that or not." 'Cause I was complaining to him, "Why me? Why me? Why did this happen to me?" And he said, "Well, it did happen to you, and now that it's happened to you and you've been given the tools to fight it, what are you going to do with it?" So, you know, I was drafted, so now I'm a foot soldier. I'm fightin' the good fight. I do it every day. Every single day.

Amy: When you go through these things and you've been hurt like this, and it does sort of break open your soul in this way, I do think that in some ways it makes you more tenderhearted towards people who are suffering, no matter what the situation is. And I think there is a potential for you to help other people who are suffering.

Janet: And there's also an ancient Chinese proverb that says, "Who should do the difficult thing? He who can." I like it. It works for me.

Nancy: Where do I find joy? With my family, my children, my grandchildren, my job. I have a job that I love, and that's being a nurse. So I feel like I can do a lot of good in the community. I'm a nurse.

Laurie: Now my pastor friends who have stayed with me—it has made them better, they say. So don't stop talking about it.

(Lights dim.)

Scene 4: God.

(Eighteen laborers are seated under the arbor in Willow's garden. Assorted day lilies and Sweet William bloom in a riot of yellow, orange, pink, white, and red. Purple coneflowers and hosta flowers add soothing color to contrast. Foliage from leaves and shrubs adds green background color. Ornamental grasses sway with the wind. A bird bath made from an offering plate sits, too, in the garden. Water sounds from the pond echo through the air. An arrangement of lavender has been placed on the center of the table.)

Narrator: *(Stage left.)* Everyone's concept of God changed as a result of their assault. Although nearly all experienced a period of doubt and atheism, with time reconnection with the Sacred occurred for many. Although a number no longer felt spiritual, laborers who felt connected to the Divine felt it more keenly than they had prior to their assault. However, some found it difficult to name this Presence. Some felt relief in freeing themselves of traditional understandings of God. *(Exits.)*

Tabitha: That's pure, that's pure God's Word. Those liturgical songs, they're not phony. They're just telling the truth. I hope when I die, I'm hearing something like that because there's nothing wrong with that. That's uncontaminated God's Word there.

Sarah: I know God more personally now and as a loving Father, not an abusive, demanding one who is waiting to strike me down if I do something wrong.

Valerie: It's more of a heavenly Father. When I do pray, I always pray to my heavenly Father for some reason, and it's not that my father was Godly at all *(laughs)*, but there's something in there that gives me a little bit of solace at this point.

Laurie: When that man tries to stick his hooha up your yahoo, I'm tellin' you, all of a sudden, God gets really personal. All of a sudden, "Jesus, I know you'd never do that to me, but did you just see what he did?" I mean, that makes my relationship way more personal. And then when Yahoo stuck his U-Haul, I thought, "Wow." So God becomes more personal. It can't just be Almighty God. It has to be Father. The word Jesus used for father is Abba, Daddy. It means running to Daddy and jumping into his lap and saying, "Daddy, did you see what that guy just did to me?" That's how it changed. God the Father was my Father I respected, loved, and then he became Daddy. "Daddy, did you see that nimrod? What the heck?"

Narrator: *(Stage left.)* For some laborers, their images of God deepened, and for some they radically changed. A few of the laborers have difficulty naming this Otherness. *(Exits.)*

Dee: The God He, the Church God, you know, that's where I was on that path . . . with God He, God She, Whoever It Is, the God of your understanding.

Susan: I can't say with conviction that I believe Jesus is the Son of God anymore. I can't even say with conviction that there is a God. I think there is. I believe in love and the greater power of love and how that can transform lives. But as a deity, you know, there's a part of me that says, "Yes, of course." And there's another part of me that says, "I don't think so." I think that God is a man-made construct that we use to help us get through whatever it is we need to get through, and by doing that, we don't have to be loving, compassionate, or even true followers of Jesus. Now, I don't have any trouble saying that I'm a follower of Jesus because I do believe in what he taught, and how he lived his life is one of the most authentic lives ever lived. But I have a very hard time calling myself a Christian because I've heard that term used as a cloak to cover so much evil, and when I put it in terms like thinking of it as a cloak, I just want to go and take a shower. And throw off this cloak and take a shower and wash off this crap that comes with it. But in a way, that's my healing, ironically. I find healing in not having to [call myself a Christian].

Willow: I am one of those people who is going to hell in a sled. To me God is much larger than their [Christian] God because the God that I have come to experience encompasses everything. My God is a large, black, Jewish woman who is gay, whose lap I can crawl into and rest. She is warm. She is comforting. She is all-loving. But where I remain, in a sense, Christian has to do with Jesus. 'Cause I haven't been willing, or I guess Jesus hasn't been willing to let me go. It's the only part of the whole Christian thing. Jesus was a cool guy. Jesus honored women. Jesus cared about other human beings.

Jane: It's more personal, interpersonal, relational. I feel that God is now bigger, more mysterious. I guess I don't need to personify him in my own image. I see him, her, it, as my ideas about what life is about. And what suffering is for has changed, too. I believe I went through this experience for some reason that I may not ever understand. Not that it should have happened or that I wouldn't want to work towards other people having it not happen, but I guess I feel like the experience really made me search deeper inside myself for what God does. Now it just feels like a very powerful presence and a source of love and healing. I don't think I have much of a dogmatic understanding of God anymore. God seems a lot bigger to me. I don't believe that I or anyone really needs a mediator between myself and God. I believe my faith about God, it's a different kind of faith. I don't believe that life is fair or it's meant to be.

Rosa: When I see people full of God's love and absence of ego, those are the closest people to God that I know. Just loving. Encompassing.

Amy: My view of people when they're born is, we're like this beautiful, clean mirror. We were born in God's image and we reflect God's love perfectly at the time of our birth. So I think God is perfect love, and we were able to reflect his love in that way as children. As we grow up, bad things happen to us and life happens to us. And in a way, that is like mud getting thrown on that mirror, and we're not able to fully reflect God's love in a way that we did at birth. And so, over time, some people have some pretty horrific things happen to them. We were born in God's image and we were born to love perfectly, and then life happens, and we were not able to do that anymore and so our mirrors get packed with mud, and in some places that mud gets packed so thick and so heavy with suffering or our own self-destructive behaviors. Life is maybe, in some ways, like mud that gets caked on pretty heavy. They say in addiction a person reaches their breaking point and some people die in the process of getting to that bottom line. So I think that, for some of us, the mud falls away because it becomes so heavy on our mirror, and we're able to again reflect some of that love that we were born with instead of hating the people that do the bad things to us. When you learn that way of looking at life and at people and what they do, then you can say, people [who] interact with you in this bad, negative way have done this because their mirror is no longer able to reflect love, and so it is all their own self-hatred. So, when people are throwing these hate messages at you, they are really just informing you how much they hate themselves, and they are not able to love you. And instead of hating them back, you can have compassion for them that their mirror is completely covered with mud, and you can respond to them rather than react.

Narrator: *(Stage left.)* Although it was difficult for Sharon to construct her own image of God because of her background in religious education, she eventually was able to find an image. This image was helpful to her until a time when she no longer needed such imagery. She shares with us now the Mary Cassatt painting that became a source of comfort to her. *(Exits.)*

Sharon: The one that I chose was called "The Bath." "The Bath" is a picture of a woman wearing a striped dress and the dress is a long dress that goes down to her feet, and she's sitting on the chair and she has a chubby little girl sitting on her lap. The little girl is wearing her underpants and she has her feet in a basin and the basin is barely bigger than her feet. And I don't know how she's going to give the little girl a bath in that basin, but that's what it's called. And then there's a big water pitcher there that is out of proportion. The water pitcher is bigger than the little girl's legs, like up to her knees, and the little girl looks like she'd be maybe three years old or so. But it's a picture that's showing mothering and caring and concern.

I was overweight all of my life, and it's something that I've struggled with my entire life. And my mother being nagging and critical and rejecting to me over that was a big obstacle in my relationship with her. But this picture of the woman, who looks to be a rather large woman, holding a chubby little girl on her lap, and the whole overall tone of the picture is love and caring and acceptance. Those were qualities that I wanted my Higher Power to have, and so I was able to look at this picture and be reminded of the characteristics that I wanted my Higher Power to have, and I thought, maybe I need to give my Higher Power a name, and I gave my Higher Power a name that was "Amanda." That was from the Spanish or the Latin root of "to love" or "loving."

Juliana: I could disconnect from my head and feel a connection to Spirit, to a spirit beyond me, which, to me, used to be God. It gave me a similar feeling, not the same but a similar feeling, of connection to an Otherness. At this point I'm not using "God" to refer to that Otherness, but sometimes would use the word "Spirit" or "Universe." At one point, I had a vision of an old, heavy-set woman in a muumuu dress with a floppy hat that came and spoke to me. I can't see her face because the floppy hat is covering her face *(laughs)*. And I don't believe that God is wearing a muumuu dress and a big, floppy hat, but it became more feminine, not necessarily feminine, but there are times when I am talking to the Universe and I have an idea of speaking to something more feminine. Not always, but a lot of times. And something very comforting, very grandmotherly-like. Not paternalistic. It's a sweet experience with this other Higher Power. And this Higher Power gives me direction. There are times when things happen; there are times when people come into my life and I think, *That is weird. Why did that* *happen? Maybe the Universe affected that.* So I give credit to this God-figure for intervening at times, which is significant in this belief structure. But beyond that, it doesn't have a lot of definition.

Amy: Too many things have happened to think that God doesn't play some significant role in my life today.

(Lights dim.)

Scene 5: Spirituality.

(The laborers, still seated in Willow's garden, are now sipping tea and eating cookies.)

Narrator: *(Stage left.)* Some of the laborers were able to find spiritual healing in a new congregation, others found it from outside traditions, and still others were unsure of how to begin the spiritual healing process. Traditional practices that were explored included Matthew Fox's creation spirituality, fundamentalist Christianity, conservative Judaism, Bible study, the Serenity Prayer, and Dr. Dan Allendar's *Wounded Heart.* Those who looked outside their faith tradition found healing in the spirituality of Eckankar, Bruno Groening, Sylvia Browne, Native American traditions, Wicca, gardening, the medicine wheel, reincarnation, the Law of Attraction, yoga, Kundalini yoga, Louise Hayes, the book *Seth Speaks*, creating the home as a sanctuary, Buddhism, energy work, and dream work.[48] *(Exits.)*

---

48 These resources were provided by the laborers during their interviews and are included as a helpful resource. Additional information

Rosa: Everybody has to find their spiritual food in their own way. I don't believe there is any one set way.

Lindsay: There's that passage in the Bible where it talks about when Jesus dies on the cross and the veil of the temple is torn in two. It's like that thick curtain or whatever. That concept was very tangible to me because while I was being abused, there was a constant barrier or a constant wall. It was always this cloud moving over me, so not only has that wall been broken down and there is no one in the way, but I could have my direct relationship with God and there wasn't someone else interfering with that. Just that breaking free and that freedom from past [chains] of bondage—if you want a picturesque view of that. I feel like that happened to me, literally.

Laurie: It doesn't touch the essence of my spirituality, which is [that] Jesus Christ is the same yesterday, today, and forever. It doesn't touch that.

Willow: A lot of my garden and my sculpture really comes out of my pain. I take something very hard, metal, and beat it into submission and recreate something pretty. Taking something barren, because when I moved here, there was virtually nothing here, and I really didn't get into the gardening until after the clergy abuse thing, and in so many ways, it's my sanctuary. People see the result of it, but so much of my garden space is my journey. It's getting rid of the weeds. It's getting rid of the nasty stuff. It is turning something that was not good and turning it into something good. And it ends up being some-

---

on energy work and dream work can be found in the "Recommended Reading" section in the back of the book.

thing that other people, when they see it, can enjoy it. They don't see what went into it. There's a whole spiritual thing that has gone into it. They can feel it. All that energy, all that energy that I used to pour into church, and after the abuse started, the energy that I poured into the relationship—it needed somewhere to go, and it went into the garden space and it went into the welding, and they became the things that I weeded out, that I chopped out and used Roundup on and other kinds of nasty chemicals, and I don't use that a lot. But sometimes you've just got to resort to that.

(Lights dim.)

Scene 6: New Me.

(The dishes have been cleared and the laborers now linger in the garden as twilight approaches.)

Narrator: *(Stage left.)* Several laborers mentioned elements of themselves that had been rebirthed to their satisfaction. *(Exits.)*

Sarah: I was not as spiritually mature as I am now. I was more dependent then on the spiritual leader for knowledge of the Bible, but now I study for myself.

Lindsay: I would say I'm a much stronger person. In the past, I was definitely to the point of being unhealthy, not having boundaries, being a people pleaser. I think now I feel much stronger to say, "That's more than I can do," or "I don't agree with that," or "I may not be able to do all of those things you may be expecting me to do," whereas in the past, I wouldn't necessarily feel like I could do that.

Janet: So there were a lot of people who thought I was crazy or I was lying because I was a woman scorned or whatever. That all changed, and now nobody's running from me.

Amy: I think that it does make you a more compassionate person, and I think it makes you in touch with the suffering of man, and now the height of my joy is felt by the depth of my pain.

Willow: I am a kinder, more understanding, more compassionate, more skeptical individual than I ever was. I am a better person, a better human being today, because of my experience. Or because of how I have recovered from my experience. Had it not been for Joe abusing and exploiting me, I would have merrily gone on being the happy little go-to-church person who didn't have an original thought in her head, who would have bought the church doctrine just because they told me, who probably would have held on to some prejudicial ideas that the church promotes, like [that] homosexuals are evil. Today, I believe that Whoever-God-Is made us, created us, as he or she wanted us to be. I am happy with who I am today. I guess that is the bottom line. That despite everything, despite how horrible this journey was at times, how sometimes I marvel that I survived and that I didn't commit suicide, to me it is a marvel that I survived and am who I am today. I'm proud of who I am today. I like who I am today. I am very happy with the woman I've become, and I wouldn't be this woman today had it not been for Joe and the wonderful folks at St. Timothy's. I don't recognize the woman I was prior to my abuse. I don't know her at all. I remember her, but I am nowhere near that woman. So that is a positive and a good thing. My garden space is a positive and a good thing. My welding sculpture is a positive and a good thing. And I doubt all those things would exist had it not been for what happened to me in 1995. In a sense, they did me a favor in forcing me on this journey because I was forced at gunpoint, in a sense, to explore outside what I had been taught, and it was a survival mechanism for me. I couldn't go back to church. It was stolen. It was taken away. And I was left in such fear of going to any other faith community. It was like, my God, if these people who I loved and who I believed loved me, if they couldn't accept me because of what happened behind the closed and locked doors of that pastor's office, then who the hell was going to? How could I ever trust anyone in the faith community if I couldn't trust these people? So the spiritual journey really started with a gun at my head because I had to do something and find out who I was in this universe, and what I was, and why I was angry at God for so long. I believe I am where I am spiritually because this is where God has left me. I am on a journey, and every decision I have made in my life has led me to this place, and it's the right place for me to be right now. There is a lot of comfort in that. You know, it takes away the blame and the shame of not only clergy sexual abuse, but any mistakes you've made, and we've all made a heck of a lot of mistakes, unless we've lived in some kind of a vacuum. All of the good decisions, all of the poor decisions, all of the things that have happened to me in my life have led me to this place where I am now, and that is a good place. So, I can look at the past with gratitude—gratitude with an edge maybe, because it's hard to be totally satisfied *(laughing)* with some things. [But] it's very freeing.

Juliana: I like myself. In this journey in the last six years, I have found the real me. I think I lived within a persona of minister and my full adoption of all that went with that and the belief system of that faith group, such that I had disconnected from a part of me, the true me. When all that got stripped away—religion, faith group, friends, community—when everything literally was gone, I had to figure out who I was. And that's been a good thing, a very good thing, and I like the person I discovered. So, would I have wanted to go through this again to have that happen? No, probably not. [But] I like me. I like who I am and I don't know if I would be as authentic a human being as I am now if I hadn't gone through what I went through and had everything taken away. Every sense of structure. Every sense of support network. Even my faith in God. When all that got ripped away, I had to figure out who I was. And I did. And I like that person, and she's a very different person than she was five years ago.

Narrator: *(Stage left.)* Although many laborers felt parts of them had been rebirthed, only three felt they had moved beyond the assault and that their lives had returned to a new normal. The other fifteen were still in various stages of the birthing process.

(Curtain closes.)

Chapter 6

Poems of the Heart

This chapter contains poems expressing and reflecting the effect that clergy sexual assault had on laborers' significant relationships. The ability of each laborer to love, despite isolation, pain, and, at times, inability to parent her children, is highlighted. Laborers were able to transcend these harsh realities, desiring to protect those they cared for from harm. The poems also reveal the strength of the laborers by demonstrating their acceptance of broken and strained relationships.

The poems were written in *vox participare*,[49] taking the exact words of each laborer as they were transcribed from her interview, eliminating most filler words, and then placing the words in free-form poetic format. If a word or phrase was needed to clarify the meaning, I enclosed it in [brackets].

---

[49] For more information see, Monica Prendergast, "The Phenomena of Poetry in Research" in *Poetic Inquiry, Vibrant Voices in the Social Sciences*, eds. Monica Prendergast, Carl Leggo, and Pauline Sameshima (Rotterdam: Sense Publishers, 2009), xxii.

Jane's Brothers and Sisters in Christ

I had been so involved.
I was a small group leader.
I had a group of people that met regularly.
There were individual people
that
I had helped during hard times.
I was involved in
outreach, mission work.

And
it was
gone
in a week.

It was just gone.

Nobody spoke to me.

It was a total shunning.

Word got around fast,
even before I reported it,
that
I was . . .ah . . . you know.

I was telling people
I wasn't going to church anymore.
I was honest about it
and
nobody ever spoke to me
again.

I mean nobody.

It was a big loss.
I thought
I had people who were really friends
based on
brothers and sisters in Christ.

So
it was a huge loss for me.

It didn't come

a p a r t

in

p
i
e
c
e
s
.

It was all

gone!

Dee's Daughter

I went to see about my daughter
to see if he had done anything to her.

That is where my rage was!

Willow's Family

This has put up a strain on my relationship
with my father and my aunt
because they don't get it.
My father thinks
that
it takes
two to tango.

His sister,
my aunt,
who I always loved and adored,
believes
it takes
two to tango.

My mother died when she was forty-six.
My dad is remarried.
My stepmother gets it.
I'm very comfortable with my stepmother.
Wish we lived closer.
She is a lovely, lovely
woman.

My brother doesn't get it.
He's my only sibling.
He doesn't get it.

It has made family relationships
extremely
difficult.
If they can't get it,
if this is a stumbling block for them,
why should I trust other people?

Juliana's Silencing Agreement

I felt shame and guilt,
and
in that [silencing] agreement
that
I'd signed
I wasn't allowed to tell
anybody
what had happened.
I had not spoken to any of my friends
not just about this
but
at all.

So I really had been

cut off

from everything I knew.

I really believe that the abuse itself for me was not what ruined my relationship with God.
(*laughs*)
To completely lose a belief in a Christian God
was
a completely unexpected outcome.
I didn't think that was going to happen when all this happened to me.
I never anticipated that
when I signed the
silencing
agreement.

I thought it was just so I could stay in the ministry later on
and
no one would find out what happened
to hold it against me
in trying to hire me
for a
pastoral job.

It's hard to talk about this.

Nancy's Children

I tried to maintain normalcy in going to church
because
I had young children at the time,
or younger children.
I still had two at home
and
the older two were in college,
so
I wanted to maintain some normalcy.

But it was very difficult for the kids
to leave the other church
because
they had friends there.

Some of them will go to church today.
And some of them won't.

Yasmine's Family

My father doesn't know.
My mom,
later on,
I had to tell her at the end.
I told her at the end.
No one in my family knew.
No one at all.
No one in the world
knew
what was going on
because
he didn't want me to tell anyone.
Later on, well,
there were some problems
when we'd talk about religion
and
I'd tell them
I don't believe in this religion anymore.
Sometimes
they'd ignore this.
They think
I'm lost
because
they still think
I'm not emotionally stable.

I'm still not quite normal
with
this problem.

I think
they're understanding,
as opposed

to what I thought.
In the beginning,
I wouldn't tell them
not only because he didn't want me to tell them
but
also because I thought
I would hurt them
because
some families don't like this.
They get hurt
or
they may hurt me
through the other big family,
my cousins and uncles.
So
this is how it is with my family.

It's

p
u

and

d
o
w
n.

But my father sometimes doesn't like to be around me
especially
when I talk about this stuff
and
this makes me feel
unloved.

Jessica's Sexual Orientation

I went to her questioning,
seeking counsel
for my sexual orientation,
so
I was in a position
where I was making myself
vulnerable
to her
around my sexual orientation
and
had no idea that she was going to do that.

And I'm sort of feeling still
like I was then
in terms of questioning things
and
being terrified of questioning.

I think for me
it's completely confusing.
The sexual orientation piece
is
completely confused.

I feel like I'm still in the same position.
I'll say to my therapist,
"I don't know which team I'm on."

But
I haven't yet figured it out
and
even though
I think that I trust my current therapist

I have a hard time exploring
the question with her
because
of what happened the last time
I explored the question.

So
I don't make any progress.

I'm just kind of stuck . . .
(*silence*)
on that part.

I feel like
I just haven't changed
at all
in how many years it's been
because
it is such a hard area for me to work on
because
of my fears.
Even if I do on a logical level
trust [that] my current therapist
is not going to take advantage of me in the same way.

This has had a huge impact on me
since that time
in terms of
being in any kind of relationship
or
dating
or
anything.

Susan's Family

We had a foster daughter going to the college
and
she did not know
that
I was the one who was the victim.
She was always calling and talking
about the talk at school
and
the things that were being said in classes
and
by the professors.

It was awful.
I was just
devastated
by it all.

My parents lived in the same town as the college.
I remember going home once
and
my aunt and uncle were there.
They were joking about
and
laughing about
this woman who
had an affair
and
later was calling wolf.
What kind of woman
is she?

And
here

I
was,
sitting
right there.
It was my family
and
I didn’t tell them.

Tabitha's Children

All three of them were just really immersed in church.
Their friends were all
church kids.
Two of our kids went to Christian school
and
I think that's what made my middle son want to be a pastor.

Now, my oldest one escaped it all.
He's still a very strong Christian young man
and
he's very careful about where he takes his family
and
he's just a very faithful person.

One of my sons
had wanted to be a pastor.
He'd gone off for pre-seminary
and
he was worried that he was doing the wrong thing.
He did go ahead and finish.
It was just really shattered.
It was just
it was just
a big
it was a big
it was just

a big spiritual mess.

He did go on and get a church
about three years ago.
I don't know if that's a good thing or not.
But I think it probably made him a better pastor,
I'm not sure.

And my middle son who's a pastor,
I don't know spiritually where he is, though.
We can't really connect when we talk about faith or spirituality
because everything's so technical and pastor language.

My daughter
doesn't want anything to do with church anymore,
especially the
Lutheran Church.

Rosa's Son

I love my son
and
we're close
but
we don't get along.
It's oil and water.
It's a very strained relationship
and
I've had a really difficult time raising him.

He's my son and he's dear to my heart
and
I've always wanted the best for him
but very unfortunately
have not really been able to provide him with the life
I think he should have had.
Because of what happened to me with the priest.

My son has been very hurt,
short-changed because of my brokenness,
because of the
exploitation by the priest.
And he has no idea how much his life has been hurt by it.
I've tried to write him letters.
It is important that this comes out.
He's a ripple effect of what happened, of the priest abusing me.

I shut myself off from the world for
many,
many
years.

At first I didn't when my son was a baby.

I was on some medications.

But then after my son was about six,
I just started to isolate more
and
more
and
more.

So he missed out on being able to be out in the real world
because
his mom was a hermit
struggling to survive financially
to keep a

roof
o
v
e
r

o
u
r

h
e
a
d
s
.

Depressed all the time,
because the medication just kept [the depression] at bay,
and then when I got off [the pills]
because they stopped working,
I was actually worse than before I took them.

Being isolated,
not having a church,
not having many friends,
not having my family to support me.
My pain
just
shutting me off.
That's what my son had to be witness to.

I just was caught up in my own physical ailments.

Thank God he had his dad,
my ex-husband,
to do something.
But really I wasn't able to give him the things that he should have been involved [in].
I wasn't able to have him be involved in a lot of sports
or
anything that required me to spend money
and
then also be responsible and disciplined enough
to get him there.

My depression from the exploitation and isolation,
it was very detrimental to him,
and
that's something he's going to have to work through
because
I wasn't able to really give him discipline.
I wasn't strong enough to say no
or
to give him limits
or
to give him consequences,
so

he got by with a lot of things
and
he was catered to
because
I didn't have anyone else watching my back.
I wasn't able to really be effective as a parent and
strong
and
to prepare him for life.

And
he has his own escape issues.
He was given a computer at ten years old
and that
was his babysitter.
He got into the world of being on the computer
and
I wasn't strong enough to really limit that
or
give him consequences.

He has an addiction to the computer, gaming, etc., etc.
He struggles to motivate himself to get and keep a job.
He has experimented with marijuana.
So a little bit into the drug world.
Not a lot.
And
he has not yet had a girlfriend.
He's 19.
I don't know,
he's going to have to have a lot more maturity before he has a relationship
and
he's hardly had any friends.
I think his relationships

have been very affected.
He has not really had,
been able to have,
very many relationships due to his insecurities.
And yeah,
the list goes
on
and
on.
There's a lot more there about
the effects of me
as far as
bringing him up
and
how much he suffered because of my
brokenness and isolation.

All the people he didn't know
because
after the exploitation happened,
I
I
I
stopped communication with so many people
that if I didn't have that happen to me
would have been a part of my son's life,
that would have
enriched him,
but because
I
X'd out
all these people
that were at the time positive influences in my life.
My son did not have positive influences in his life.

My family
didn't step in to help me out.
I was left alone with that whole burden.
No village.
It's not fair.
It's really not fair.
It's just,
I can't get those years back.
I can't give those years back to my son.

That priest has no idea,
and even if he did, what good would it do?
You know?
You can say all the sorrys you want.
It doesn't replace those years that my son had to suffer.
It's one thing about myself,
but
HE
deserved
a lot better.

So I never can repay,
I can never give those back.
And it breaks my heart,
to see his struggles,
to not take responsibility for the whole problem,
all his challenges.
But I do take responsibility
for a lot of it
because I was his environment.
You know,
he should have had better.

(sigh)

It's part of his life path.
I have my struggles,
but still,
life's not fair.
It's just . . .
pretty horrible.

It's
really
horrible.

Laurie's Relationships

Now you have to remember
in my frame of mind
this is a man of power.
He has power over me.
He's my boss.
He's got power over me.
He's my pastor.
He's got power over me.
He's helping me with my ordination.
And I love him and his wife and his children and his dog.
They were my friends.
And
he's way **bigger** than I am.

So add all those things up,
and
when the "wonderful" men in collars were questioning me,

"Why didn't you say no?"

You know, that's easy for you guys to say.
You're not five-two
and
looking at that man in power
in all those capacities over
me.

Yeah,
I could have kicked him
if that would have been my thought,
but
I was thinking of other things

of how this was affecting my life.

After it happened, I didn't tell a soul.

And this is how it affects relationships.
I started to drink more.
One night at a local bar,
the bartender, a married man who was my friend,
said,
"It looks like you're troubled and if you want to stay after when
I close up and talk,
why don't we do that."
So I waited 'til one.
He closed the bar down
and
he came over.
We were talking.
Then he started to kiss me
and
tug at my pants.

I thought,
"Seriously?"

Then his wife,
who [had] just had a baby and lived across from the bar,
came to the door,
wondering why he wasn't home.

At that point I just thought,

"I'm just going to leave. I'm going to leave town."

So I went home
and
threw all my belongings into the car.
I drove to another resort where I spent the weekend.
Then I drove home to my family.

I just left town.
I never went back.

I explained how it went with relationships.

I drank more,
and
when I came back here to live with my family,
everyone wondered why I moved.
I didn't tell my parents.
I didn't tell my sisters or my brothers.
They wanted to know
but
I didn't want to share.
And they asked for years what happened.
I'm moving on.
You don't need to know.

It was devastating to me to lose the path I was on.
It was the best place I had ever lived,
Physically ~ by the water, hiking, in great shape!
Mentally ~ challenged at resort and in church, pondering ordination!
Emotionally ~ friends, colleagues, interaction!
Spiritually ~ working in the church to serve my God!
I had a fun job at a resort.
I enjoyed all the seasons.
There just wasn't a down-side up there.

When you're on a mountaintop,
there's someone just waitin' to push you off.
Maybe I should have been lookin'.
I just remember
it's so funny
when he was on top of me
I know what all the books say.
I know what women are supposed to do
but I'm thinking,
"This man is in so many positions of power over
me."

But it was just a total blackout when I came home.

A family member was going through a nasty divorce
and
so the family was very focused on that.
We're a very close family,
and we were very focused on that.
So it was pretty easy for me to focus
all my energy
and
all my rage
and
throw myself 24/7 into fixing
that mess.
A mess that didn't personally involve

ME.

Janet's Daughter

She's anti-religion right now
so
I don't want to dredge it up
because
I am hoping that the more time goes by,
the more it stays in the past
maybe
she'll start having some sort of a relationship with G-d.

I don't really care what form it takes.
I just want her to be spiritual in some way other than through the environment,
which is what she's doing right now.

She believes in G-d, but that's where it stops.
We're working on that
very
gently.

I have hope.

It really impacted her.
That is something I will never forgive him for.

I hope he never walks in front of my car.
I just want him to stay away from me.
I don't know how I would react.
I could react quite badly.
Knee him in the
nards
at the very least.

And it's not for me.
It's for my child.

I'm an adult.
I can take care of myself,
but

LOOK!

what you did to my

daughter!

Sharon's Parents and Friends

I can see [that]
my relationship with Joe
irreparably
changed the course of my life.

Because
there was this obstacle
with my parents,
my friends.

What happened with him
altered relationships
that
were extremely important to me
that
I could never get back.
And so
that makes
me angry now.
It makes me very angry—

My inability in myself
to put the relationships on the line
by stating what had happened,
letting
my parents and my friends
really know me
for who I was.
I felt like having some relationship
with those people
even though it was superficial
meant more to me

than taking the risk
of
alienating
them
to the extent that the relationships might end,
which
was what
I thought
was a good chance would happen.

Willow's Sons

My youngest son,
Jason,
wanted to be a pastor.

Both my boys idolized this
asshole!

Their worlds were turned
I
N
S
I
D
E

O
U
T

&

U
P
S
I
D
E

D
O
W
N
!

They wanted Jason to go to camp for the weekend.
It was a place for them to tell Jason
what an
asshole
his mother was.
Jason hasn't shared everything of that experience.

Jason wants nothing
ABSOLUTELY
NOTHING
to do with anything church.

Jason,
I don't think he's religious at all.
We don't talk about it.

Samuel
has turned into a party animal.
Samuel wants nothing to do with it.
Samuel still believes in God
and
still believes in some of that stuff.
He's kind of Christian in name.
Like when you're filling out an application,
they ask what your religion is.
That's probably as religious as he is.
We don't talk about it.

My sons
understand I was abused.
That's probably why they don't have anything to do with the church
because
they don't blame me.

They blame the church
for the way
the church
treated
us!

Valerie's Son

And the sticky situation is
that my son remained friends with Joe,
and
there were a few times
when I went to visit and to see
my son and his family,
and
they invited this guy to come over!

I certainly wasn't going to tell my son not to
because
he would want to know why.

And I have not had the strength to tell him about it.
He would probably be so angry
I couldn't guarantee you what he would do
or
how he would act
to this guy
at all.

I've kept my own secret about it from him.

I don't feel good about that.

This guy even was coming on to me
the last time I was visiting
[and] they invited him to come over.
I did tell my son that he did not have to invite Joe over just
because I was there.

I said,
"As a matter of fact,
I'd rather spend the time with you and your family
and
not have him come."
And he said,
"Well, what's going on?"
And I said,
"Well, he's, um, tried to hit on me a couple of times and I don't appreciate that."
And his attitude was,
"Oh, Mom, come on, get with it."
Of course, he didn't know anything that had happened,
so I guess he was telling me to go out and have a good time.

(laughs)

But he didn't
know.
No,
no,
no!
He didn't
know.

I'm glad now that my son doesn't invite him over at all when I'm there.
That's been wonderful.
It was,
it was,
it was
extremely difficult for me
not to lose my temper
and
probably pop him a few times

and
knock him out.
(laughs)

I haven't had to see him now for a few years.
So that helps a lot.

Amy's Children

I said,
"Well, we have to say something to the children."
And so we went out to the kids,
who were getting lunch prepared.
And I said,
"Look, I'm having a nervous breakdown . . ."
. . . and my daughter started crying.

My oldest son had such a difficult time.
He loved the pastor, too.

(cries)

And
so he had his own struggles
dealing with the fact that
the pastor had done something to his own mother.
And so
he really hated him.
And
instead of being able to confront that figure and deal with that,
he got involved in drugs.
He would just self-medicate.
He had a lot of kids he went to church with,
and
they just acted like nothing happened.
And I can remember one day
my son coming home from high school
and he said,
"I saw the **prick** at school today."

"Oh, really? What was he doing?"

"He was teaching something after school."

"What happened?"

"He said hello and acted like nothing was wrong."

So my son,
I don't know what level of shame he experienced in regard to that,
but I'm sure there had to be a great deal for him
and
my other two children.

And it was painful for the kids to be around their dad dealing with his pain
and
it was difficult to be knowing that their mother had done what she had done.
And I imagine they felt some
shame
as people knew about it.

I believe that my daughter was sexually assaulted
by the minister also.
She had gone to a hospital because she was cutting herself.
She was hurting and in a lot of pain
and
I just couldn't physically take care of the kids
and at the time
my husband seemed like the better parent to take the kids
and yet
as it turned out
he was having a great physical time too.

I had nothing left to give to my children.

I was not capable of taking care of my children
in any
way,
shape,
or
form.
I couldn't even take care of myself
hardly.

My ex-husband
in all his
own suffering through this
had a
great,
difficult time
taking care of his own emotional state of mind, too,
and he was getting his own help, counseling,
and
he insisted that the children go to counseling.

They did for a time
but
my daughter really resented it,
my oldest refused to go,
and the middle child went.

Eventually, because my daughter was cutting so much, she
ended up in the hospital
a couple of times.
That is when she brought up the fact that the minister had
sexually assaulted her.
And the way that she said it,
they thought she was just doing it to identify with me.
They didn't really believe her

and
they claimed that they couldn't find him
and
they didn't know where he was
and
so
they weren't going to push to any criminal action
because
legally that is a crime.
And I thought they were obligated to report that to the local authorities
and
I felt like they just didn't believe her.

She talked to me about this years later
and
I really believe that he did do that
because
I don't think she could make up a story like that.

My middle child is probably the least affected
because
he has a very nonchalant way of living life.
He kind of just accepts things as they go along
and
he muddles through
and
he just manages.
He seems, emotionally,
the most stable of all my children.

And so my kids,
they learned to find ways to cope.

They, for a time, went to church

because
their dad went
and
made them go.
And my older son,
he just refused to have anything to do with it.
I think he missed it
but
he was still very angry at the pastor.

After I had left,
they would get in very physical fights
and
my middle child would leave
and
my daughter would participate in her own self-destructive
behavior
and
my oldest son would fight back
And would become extremely angry
and
then would run away and go be with friends.
Eventually my daughter ran away from home.

(sighing)

I have to respect the fact that my kids
have their journey to walk, too.
Sadly
their journey is connected by some
really horrific thing
that happened to all of us
together,
not just me.
They have to find their way.

The only thing I can do
is to pray for my children
and
ask God to protect them
and
hope that the fact that I don't do that every single day
still means that somehow God will
watch over them and protect them.

Because
we go down the path that we go down
with the abuse,
I wonder if our children don't at some level
feel we betrayed them as much as we were betrayed.
And in a sense, through no fault of our own,
we were gone from ourselves,
we were not available emotionally
and
physically
and
spiritually
to be present to our children
because
we were lost in our own
pain
and
suffering.

Rosa's Kids

I didn't have [more] kids
because
I had to go on the medication
because
of the exploitation,
and
that's all I ever wanted
was to have a lot of kids.

(laughs)

That's all I dreamed about.

Susan's Children

My children are agnostic.
They don't go to church.
I'm proud of them.
I'm proud
that
they are just not swallowing
anything
and
everything.

They are very
thoughtful,
compassionate,
and
caring
young adults now.
They are both in college.

Well,
I have a daughter who is 18
who has Down syndrome.
I would say she's not affected at all.
Nothing much affects her.
As long as she is
loved
and
secure,
she
is
happy.

But the other two
saw what I went through at the church
and
they basically said,
"No,
it's not for us."

Angela's Family

Actually
my children have been stronger in the faith,
probably more so than I have.
But of course you know
we're dealing with a situation
where, because of his lie,
everything else gets overshadowed.
So the church is trying to protect this pastor

and
they forgot
about my husband who needed to be talked to.

They forgot
about my children who needed to be talked to.

Do you see what I'm saying?

One of the pastors said,
"We have to protect this man
AT ALL COST."

And
"at all cost" meant protecting this man
at the expense of my children,
who needed counseling,
and
my husband, who needed the friendship of all these men
who called themselves
brother
for the last thirteen years.
And so, yes, it affected them.

My kids
even asked me,

(laughs)

"Can we talk to them
if we see somebody from the ex-church?"
Because
there [are] a few groups of people that have
just totally
100 percent
turned their back on us.

And on top of that,
the other thing
that is just devastating in life
is that nobody called us to ask us our side of the story.
So my kids
[are] much stronger than I am
because
they've got a dad.
My husband talks to them
over
and
over
again.

Now my daughter,
number two,
you can't talk to her.
She gets so angry about the whole situation.
You can't talk to her about it.
You can't say anything to her about it.
And so we need to get her through some counseling.
And all that gets overshadowed by the pastor and his lies.

I'm not doing good.
My husband is trying to talk to me.
I've got the other two that have forgiven me.
But like I said,
my middle daughter,
she still struggles with it.
I accept that from her.
It's really hard.

But all of us
are still waiting for *us*
to be at church.
Because
we want to be at church
as a *family* again.

And my daughters,
they'll go visiting churches.
They'll just go visit.
I haven't even gone and visited any church at all this winter.
Since probably November.
It's been a long time.

My Children

An atheist
and
two agnostics.

Three children of Creation,
dearly loved.

Sarah's Husband

During the abuse,
my husband and I fought quite a bit.

Once, he suspected what was going on
and
later discovered his worst fears.
He knew that it was abuse.

Afterward,
my husband confronted the pastor.

It was spiritually devastating
for both
me and my husband.

He always recognized it as abuse,
but
it had the appearance of an affair
at times,
and
since I could not see things clearly
at the time,
it led to many arguments.

My husband always tried to be
very supportive and
helpful to me,
even though
he was hurting so much himself.

I would not have lived without God's intervention
and
my husband's love and care for me.

Amy's Grandchildren

So when my first grandchild was born
I was literally in love with this baby
and
I had to pinch myself.
I have a grandbaby!
I have a baby that came from *my own child.*
It's a baby that's connected to *me* in this way.
It was such a profound feeling.
And when I am with my granddaughters today,
when I babysit with them
and
play with them,
I love them so much.
I feel like I love them so **big.**
I enjoy so much being with them
and
when I hold them in my arms
it feels so good in my body and my heart.
I love them so **big** like that.
It's the only way I can describe them is
I love them so big.
And
in some strange way
it's like loving myself all over again
and
loving parts of myself,
being able to love them in this way,
to play with them,
to have the joy of being able to walk to the door
and

have them see me
and
be so happy to see me.

This gives me great joy!

Lindsay's Advice to Support People

One issue
that
I would have liked to have more of was
support people.
Even if they aren't survivors.
Even if they just have a heart to minister to [survivors].

Right when this initially started
I had different people
bombard me with,
"Okay, you have to go to counseling now."
And "There's going to be a trial."

And it was all thrown to me at once.

It wasn't really my decision.

I have a lot of people say,
"Well, let me know if you need anything."
or
"If there's anything I can do to help you...."

Well,
when people were offering,
I didn't know what to say.
I didn't know what I was going to need
and
I didn't know really how to ask.
I'm not a very assertive person,
so
it wasn't very beneficial
because
when I did need things,

I didn't really feel like
a couple of months later
I could go back to these people
and
say,
"Remember, you volunteered to help.
Could you do this for me?"
I kind of felt like that was definitely
out of my comfort zone
to do that.

So
I would have liked
to have had people offer
a little bit later
in my healing process,
when
I would have been able to say,
"Well, if you'd like to help,
this would be something that
would really encourage and be helpful to me."

Amy on Children and Laborers

I wish they could teach children how to love themselves
'cause
that's the key to life.
Because if you can love yourself
and
learn how to forgive yourself,
then those are the keys to living.

Because even though we are victims of clergy abuse,
we victimize ourselves
in some sense.
We blame ourselves for putting ourselves in those situations.
We blame ourselves for saying yes [when] we should have said no.
We blame ourselves for being in the wrong place at the wrong time.

We have to be able to forgive ourselves.
I think,
more than forgiving the predator preacher
that did these things,
we have to be able to forgive ourselves.

Then we have to take good care of ourselves
and
we have to love ourselves.
If we are able to love ourselves,
then that is when we are able to have compassion.
We're able to respond to people
that are hurt around us.
We're able to respond in appropriate ways,
respond with compassion
and

not to take these things and be self-destructive,
hurt ourselves,
and
hurt other people who are around us.

Instead we can become the women
we were all intended to be—
the way we were when we were first born,
the perfect love that God was—
and
love other people.
That is what really matters.

I try to tell these things to my children
but they are not ready to hear them,
and
not all people are ready to hear them.

All you can do is hope that at some point
you'll say it at a time when someone is able to hear it,
and
they'll be able to grow and become better people
and
have forgiveness for themselves
and
learn how to love themselves.

Chapter 7

My Night Journey

In 2003, Joe had been my pastor for eight years. During that time, I had grown to trust and respect him. I was a seminarian and was working as the Youth and Family Minister at the church. He was my mentor, and for several months had been serving as my spiritual director as I prepared for the ordination process.

Shortly before the assault, Pastor Joe asked to read my psychological profile that had been done as a routine part of the candidacy process for ordination. At the time of the psychological testing and assessment, I had been told—again, as a matter of routine—not to share the contents of it with anyone because the contents could be used to hurt me. When Joe asked for the profile, I was hesitant, but I convinced myself that because he was spiritually directing me, it would show distrust in the counseling relationship if I refused. "Besides," I reasoned, "something in the report may help with my spiritual direction."

Then one night, I was in angst over my sense of call to serve the church. After talking to my husband about my struggle, he suggested I email Joe. The next morning Pastor Joe called and told me he had received my email the previous night, had been thinking of me all night, had cancelled all his morning appointments, and would be over to my house in an hour.

After hanging up, I freaked! My husband and kids had just left for the day, my house was messy with cereal bowls still out, and I was in my pajamas. As I flew around the house, getting ready for Pastor Joe's arrival, my stomach was in knots because I couldn't help but think, "I must be worse off than I believed if he thought about me all night and canceled his morning appointments in order to see me." His overreaction to my email had turned my angst into a crisis of epic proportion. By the time he arrived, I was close to hysterics.

At my house that morning, Joe comforted me by holding my hand and hugging me. He had never done this before. A few days later, he told me that he knew my spiritual call was to form a "spiritual partnership" with him, similar to the partnerships shared between St. John of the Cross and St. Teresa of Avila[50], and between St. Francis and St. Clare of Assisi.[51] Both sets of saints are said to have had close, platonic, professional relationships similar to Gertrude Stein and Ernest Hemingway or Virginia Woolf and Lytton Strachey. After he told me of our spiritual partnership, he held me close, embracing me tightly.

---

50 St. Teresa of Avila lived in the 1500s in Spain and was the founder of the Discalced (Barefoot, or Sandaled) Carmelites, an order for both female and male religious. St. John of the Cross became Teresa's spiritual director, or confessor, and helped her reform the Carmelite order by founding Discalced Carmelite monasteries and convents. Cathleen Medwick, *Teresa of Avila: The Progress of a Soul*, (New York: Doubleday, 1999).

51 In the early 1200s, St. Francis, of the town of Assisi in Italy, founded a monastic order that was first called "the order of lesser brothers," and which today is known as the Franciscan religious order. St. Clare of Assisi founded a sister order known as the "Poor Clares." These orders were based on poverty and identification with the poor. Justo Gonzales, *The Story of Christianity, Volume 1,* (San Francisco: Harper, 1984), 302-306.with the poor. Justo Gonzales, *The Story of Christianity, Volume 1,* (San Francisco: Harper, 1984), 302-306.

Two days later, I walked into Joe's office to return a book I had borrowed. Abruptly, he stood and kissed me, saying, "That was the kiss of peace practiced by the ancient Christians." He then led me to the sanctuary, where he took my left hand and inspected my bridal rings, saying, "You know I will never do anything to hurt your marriage. Tell me the story of how you were given your engagement ring."

Not long after that, he raped me in his office. Afterward, he jumped up and euphorically shouted, "You really wanted that! I could tell how much you wanted that! Now get dressed and leave. I need to think about what just happened."

Nauseated, I left his office in shock, thinking, "What just happened? How did I get through high school and college without something like this happening and now I'm a married woman, who loves her husband, and this thing just happened in the pastor's office?"

I was never the same person again.

The Stockholm Syndrome

The rape emotionally bonded me to Joe in what is known as the Stockholm Syndrome.[52] The Stockholm Syndrome

---

[52] The Stockholm Syndrome was first documented in 1973, after two bank robbers took four people hostage for one hundred thirty-one hours. The hostages bonded with their captors in ways counter to what was perceived to be normal. "They showed support for their captors and shielded them from the police. Afterwards, they refused to testify against them, raised money for their defence and even visited them in prison." The Stockholm Syndrome is noted not only in hostage situations, but also in other circumstances of abuse, such as domestic violence. Pat Wallace, "How Can She Still Love Him? Domestic

occurs when a "trauma bond" develops between a victim and his or her abuser. Rev. Dr. Thomas P. Doyle contends that people sexually victimized by a clergyperson often exhibit the characteristics of the Stockholm Syndrome.[53] Four conditions must be present for the Stockholm Syndrome to ensue: [54]

1. *"Perceived extreme threat to physical or psychological survival"*

My assault and subsequent rape were perceived as a threat to my physical and psychological well-being.

2. *"Perceived inability to escape"*

Doyle writes that clergy abuse victims are often "paralyzed and numb with fear when the abuse [occurs] because of their disbelief that so sublime a personage would stoop to harm them."[55] This was true for me. I explicitly trusted Joe, and when he began crossing physical boundaries, I did not equate it with abuse. In fact, I was not able to understand the relationship as abusive until two years after it had ended! However, the morning after he told me we were called to a spiritual relationship, and before either the kiss or the rape, I wrote in my journal, "My heart is heavy. I finished the bottle of wine and walked to the store and bought another bottle. I

Violence and the Stockholm Syndrome," *Community Practitioner* 80, no. 10 (2007), 32.

[53] Marianne Benkert and Thomas P. Doyle, "Clericalism, Religious Duress and Its Psychological Impact on Victims of Clergy Sexual Abuse," *Pastoral Psychology* 58 (2009), 223-238.

[54] Wallace, "How Can She Still Love Him?", 33.

[55] Benkert and Doyle, "Clericalism," 232.

finished half of it but could not bring myself to eat. I awoke during the night. I am terrified to go to church tomorrow morning." I was terrified, yet at the same time "paralyzed" to act because I could not think of any concrete action to take. I had always known Joe as a well-respected pastor, not only toward me but in the community in which we lived. Who would I tell? What would I say? I did not even have a conscious idea of what was transpiring. I was going through a "crisis of epic proportions," and he was the stable one. Shortly after this, I stopped keeping a journal.

3. *"Isolation from perspectives other than that of the captor/perpetrator"*

Joe isolated me from my support people by telling me he was the only one who understood my spirituality, as we had been destined to work together as a "spiritual couple." He isolated me from my husband David by making comments implying that David did not have the theological background to help me spiritually. He implied that I was too old to rely on my mother for emotional support and that I needed to break the "childlike bond" (in his words) which I had with her. In addition, he told me not to breathe a word of what had happened to my friends in the church because, he said, the relationship would destroy the church. He then proceeded to meet individually and privately with my friends, sharing the news of our "spiritual partnership" with them. To this day, I have no idea what he said because the friends he spoke with will no longer associate with me. Finally, Joe said the bishop was an incompetent man with no backbone and could not be trusted. Joe's saying and doing these things led me to become distrustful of everyone and completely dependent on him.

4. *"Perceived small kindnesses from the captor/ perpetrator"*

Although Joe's behavior was abusive and made my life a living hell, he also paid me compliments in areas where I had previously felt inadequate, such as telling me I was a gifted public speaker. Small compliments like these were enough to make the entire relationship seem worthwhile to me, especially since others were noticing my strange behavior and questioning what my problem was.

If the four conditions of the Stockholm Syndrome have been met, four resulting beliefs and behaviors may emerge: [56]

1. *"An overwhelming need to pacify the [perpetrator] "*

Joe's needs became a priority and usurped the needs of my family and me. Never before had I placed anything above the needs of my family, especially in regard to my children. Yet it became extremely important to me to appease Joe. Prior to this, I had never had the need to placate anyone.

2. *"Survivor adopts the captor's/perpetrator's perspective of the world"*

My ability to think critically and for myself evaporated. I believed every far-fetched theory Joe told me about our relationship because what he said attached meaning to the abuse. In adopting his bizarre worldview, I held suspect all other perspectives. Never before had I had trouble thinking for myself, nor had I ever held suspect everyone else's viewpoints.

---

[56] Wallace, "How Can She Still Love Him?", 33.

3. *"Intense feelings of gratitude toward the [perpetrator] "*

I was thankful to God for calling me into this "spiritual partnership" with Joe, despite the turmoil it caused in my life. I was thankful for Joe. The relationship and Joe became the only important aspect of my life.

4. *"[Survivor] rejects offers of help or rescue, which [she perceives] could aggravate the [perpetrator] "*

My husband and my mother tried to get me to see that my relationship with Joe was not healthy and that he was manipulating me, but I literally could not understand them when they spoke frankly to me. I remember thinking, "I know what they are saying used to make sense and I used to believe that stuff, but I just don't understand their logic anymore." It was almost as if they were speaking a foreign language.

After sixteen months, my marriage was nearly broken and I could no longer stand the wretched lifestyle I was living. I told my husband about the sexual relationship with Joe. Joe turned himself in to the bishop. The assaultive relationship ended. We both lost our jobs. I nearly lost my marriage. I was left a shell of the person I had been prior to the abuse.

My Ascent from Darkness

I realized this book needed to be written shortly after I graduated from seminary in 2006. At that time, I was nearing the two-year anniversary of the end of my sexual assault and had recently recognized the relationship as abusive. I was struggling with not being able to find a safe congregation to attend. The loss of my congregation, many friends, and my career in the church paled in comparison to the loss of my spiritual self. Scripture, meditation, hymns, holidays, and sacred pictures triggered post-traumatic stress.

I longed to connect with other women who had lived through clergy sexual assault so I could learn from their experiences and, in the process, find some relief from my own soul wound. I had sought such women through my denomination, but was told on several occasions that they were not able to connect me with other women because women who have been sexually victimized by clergy do not want to be contacted by the church.

But this was not my experience. I *wanted* to be contacted by the church. I wanted to know I mattered to someone in my denomination. I left my name and contact information with several denominational leaders in case another woman so victimized should request a friend. I was never contacted.

In my isolation, I often sobbed deeply into my pillow after my husband and children had left for the day. How could I find my way out of this mess without the support of a mentor who had lived through it? How could I do it when my friends were shunning me? How could I do it without a connection to God?

In the past when I had struggled with grief, such as the three times I miscarried, I was able to work through my grief because my faith sustained me. I had the support of everyone who knew about my loss. I was mentored by other mothers who had miscarried. In fact, on the first Mother's Day after I miscarried, before I had any children, I received a carnation at church. When I protested that I was not a mother, I was told that I was indeed a mother. This support and nurturing helped me find my way through the pain and grief of my miscarriages.

But clergy sexual assault is not accepted like miscarriage. After my assault was disclosed to the congregation, I received anonymous hate mail and was accosted in public, in front of my children, by some in my church family. I stayed home as much as I could. When I did venture out, I constantly scanned the horizon, alert to who was in the vicinity, always aware of the possibility of being ambushed with venomous words or, worse yet, being looked at and ignored.

I struggled with the shame of sexual violation, feelings of stupidity for being victimized, uncontrollable rage at the offender for manipulating me, the stressors of living with PTSD, abandonment by my brothers and sisters in Christ, the loss of many friendships that were important to me, the loss of my career, and the guilt of hurting my husband, children, parents, and friends. It also pained me to observe the spiritual bewilderment of my children. Trapped in my own spiritual darkness, I was at a loss as to how to guide their spiritual development. The church had been prominent in their lives and mine, and now it was gone. We were mourning.

During the period of the assault and its immediate aftermath, I could barely function. I could not care for my children. I could not even clean my house. I suffered from visual and auditory hallucinations. The hallucinations gradually ceased after the assaultive relationship ended, and little by little, I was able to resume daily activities. During this time of early recovery, I would call my husband at work to give him a report of my daily accomplishments: “Guess what I just did? I folded a load of laundry!” “I took a walk with the kids!” “I made lunch!” He would respond supportively, “That’s wonderful!”

Every little step I took toward normalcy was like a step up Mount Everest. My husband’s encouragement allowed me to focus on the small steps I had taken rather than the million more steps I needed to take to reach the level where I had previously functioned. His willingness to meet me where I was, to encourage me in my small successes, and to hear my innermost pain was paramount to my recovery. Eventually, I reached a place where I could hear *his* pain and his feelings of betrayal. His support and our sharing brought us closer than we had been in the previous fifteen years of our marriage.

But I still longed for a friend who had been through clergy sexual assault and could mentor me in light of our shared experience. Two years after the assaultive relationship ended, my denomination was still unable to connect me with other laborers, so I created a website for laborers from my denomination. My hope was not only to find a friend, but to learn that the harsh treatment I had experienced on the part of church leaders was an isolated incident. My site was up for ten months; during that time, twenty laborers longing for connection sent me request forms.

After receiving a number of these emails, I asked to be placed on my synod's Clergy Misconduct Response Team; my aim was to help ensure that no other woman would experience the inept denominational response that had been inflicted on me and on those who had contacted me through my website. My request to help was denied. I had also come up with several healing ideas the church could implement, such as offering a survivors retreat, an online support group, or laborers presenting their stories to denominational leaders or seminarians. When I presented these ideas, intended to help women heal, to a representative responsible for misconduct prevention in my denomination, she responded that she would have to consult with the denomination's lawyers before providing an answer. Each time, my idea was found implausible. Eventually, I was told by the representative who is responsible for misconduct prevention that the church did not need volunteers.

At this same time, I was struggling to find a congregation to attend. At each of the four congregations my family and I sought to attend, we were shamed in some way by a clergyperson. We were even formally expelled at one. After this instance, I sought church mediation with the minister who expelled us. I felt emotionally and psychologically strong going into the mediation, so I went alone. The mediator was an ordained pastor in my denomination who was also a doctoral-level therapist and a member of my synod's Clergy Misconduct Response Team. When I arrived, he was making social plans with the minister who had expelled me from her congregation. During mediation, the mediator was inappropriate on several occasions by asking me questions such as, "Has Joe's wife called to thank you?"

"Thank me for what?" I responded.

"Because Joe is now better in bed," he replied.

This line of questioning detracted from the mediation by triggering me, and I shut down by dissociating. From that point on, I was unable to stand up for myself and negotiate with the minister who had issued the expulsion. Had my therapist, my spiritual director, or a trained advocate been present, they could have ended the mediation, removed me from the situation, and offered me support immediately following the retraumatizing event.

Due to being retraumatized at these four churches, by my denomination, and during mediation, I decided I was not yet strong enough to deal with the reality I had learned through my website, that the collusion I was experiencing was not an isolated incident but was widespread throughout the national church. Since I could not yet handle the truth that women were treated so cavalierly by the denomination I loved and to which I had devoted my life, I chose to delete my website.

Yet, the ten months of owning the website had taught me three important things: First, the women who contacted me longed for friendships with other laborers. Second, they desired that church leaders recognize how badly they had been violated. Third, most seemed just as confounded as I was about how to heal spiritually. Often, these women lamented that there was a lot of information about what clergy sexual assault is, but nothing available on how to heal spiritually.

After deleting my website, I attended a retreat sponsored by the Healing Alliance for people who had been abused by clergy. One of the women at the retreat suggested I write a book on spiritual healing. I thought about this but decided I would never do clergy abuse advocacy again unless someone in a position of authority approached me specifically to do so, because I felt it was no longer healthy for me to put myself in a position to be rejected by those in the church.

Shortly thereafter, I completely withdrew from the church and everything having to do with clergy sexual assault. I went into my darkest night of the soul because the rejection by my denomination, my friends, and the clergy in my community was too much to bear. I stopped seeing my spiritual director and my therapist. I no longer had any energy to work on healing my soul wound. I was convinced I was an atheist. This depressed me. All sense of joy in life was missing. My soul was dead to me, for who was I if I had devoted my life to serving God and there was no God?

By all outer appearances, I was functioning well, working full-time as a department head at the local YMCA. My relationships with my husband, my children, and my parents were stronger than ever. I was forming new friendships at my job, but fitness had never been the passion that spirituality and social justice had been for me. I felt I was going through the motions of existence rather than truly living. Sometimes when my pain grew too strong, I would flee to the restroom at work to cry. I had always been a very spiritual person and I did not want to give the offender the power to take that away from me. The spiritual void in my life was ever-present and incredibly painful. My deepest desire was to heal spiritually, but I had no idea how to do that, so I succumbed to the dark void within and busied myself with many activities, including joining Toastmasters International.

Almost without my realizing it, Toastmasters gradually became a community of healing. I first told the story of my assault publicly at a Toastmasters meeting. When I finished my first speech on clergy sexual assault, the club members applauded and gave me positive feedback. That empowered me to speak on clergy sexual assault at other events.

Over the course of speaking publicly about clergy sexual assault, I learned that the way in which the assault is disclosed to the congregation impacts how congregants respond to a laborer. For example, when church leaders use the phrase, "The pastor had a sexual relationship with an adult member of the congregation," or "The pastor engaged in sexual misconduct with a woman in the congregation," it implies to congregants that the pastor and the virgin had a consensual sexual relationship. After I started speaking on clergy sexual assault, several people from the congregation where my assault took place approached me and said, "I'm sorry. I never knew the truth about what happened to you." This convinces me that it is crucial to attach a term like "sexual assault" to the act when the abuse is disclosed; when the word "assault" is used, few will assume the relationship was a consensual love affair.

Life continued. In many respects it was very good. The void was still present, but I had learned how to enjoy myself despite its constant intrusiveness. Five years after the assaultive relationship had ended, my daughter, who is a musician, was asked to play at a local church service the Sunday before Christmas. Ever since the assault, I had struggled with Christmas. But it had been five years, and I had not been triggered with post-traumatic stress for many months. I had not been to church in several years and was eager to try going to a new denomination. I love Christmas carols and sing them all year long, so I decided to go and hear Abby play her clarinet. Our fifteen-year-old exchange student, who had been itching to go to an American church service, went with me.

About ten minutes into the service, I started having flashbacks. I changed my breathing pattern and focused on my surroundings by mentally naming what I was taking in with my senses in an attempt to ground myself in the present moment and thereby halt the flashbacks. I thought I had everything under control but realized I did not when our exchange student leaned over and whispered, "Carolyn, are you all right?"

Without realizing it, I was noisily shaking my bulletin and breathing loudly. I whispered, "No," stood up, and ran down the aisle.

Once outside the sanctuary, I threw myself face-down on the floor in the narthex and sobbed loudly. I became aware that our exchange student had followed me out when I felt her hand on my back and heard her timidly ask again, "Carolyn, are you all right?"

As much as I wanted to berate myself for missing my daughter's first gig and for falling apart in front of our exchange student and a congregation where I knew no one, I refused to go down that road. After all, do we berate ourselves when our throat hurts? When we stumble and fall? Then why berate ourselves for having a public post-traumatic stress episode?

I lifted my head from the floor. Hyperventilating, I said between breaths, "I haven't . . . acted like this . . . in a long . . . time . . . I'll be okay. . . . Something bad . . . happened to me . . . in church. . . . I guess . . . it still . . . makes me sad."

She looked at me with wide eyes and said, "It must have been really bad."

Between deep gulps of air, I said, "Yes, it was. Let's get out of here and go get some hot chocolate and cookies while we wait for Abby to be done."

Other than this event, Christmas that year was filled with more joy than the four that preceded it. Shortly thereafter in early 2009, I learned I had been accepted into a Master's of Social Work program at Grand Valley State University in Grand Rapids, Michigan. Although it excited me to finally discover a career path I might be able to embrace with some enthusiasm, a part of me was angry at having to start over with a career and having to pay for a second master's degree. The same week I received the acceptance letter, I also received a phone call from Baylor University in Waco, Texas, asking me if I would be interested in becoming a spokesperson for their research on clergy sexual misconduct of adult women; I had participated in the research several months earlier. I readily agreed and, along with several other women, was flown to Baylor University for media training.

At Baylor, I truly felt accepted, and in some way, this acceptance freed me from much of the guilt and shame I had been carrying regarding my assault. The Baylor team, led by Dr. Diana Garland, took what had happened to us seriously and had even hired a public relations firm to teach us how to tell our stories to the media. While at Baylor, I learned that the School of Social Work had conducted the research on clergy sexual misconduct, and it dawned on me that social work was a field in which research and advocacy around clergy sexual assault were acceptable. Though I didn't recognize it at the time, when I left Baylor, a pivotal piece of my healing had begun.

In September 2009, under Baylor University, I began sharing my story with the press. In doing so, I came to realize how healing it is to share one's story and actually have it heard and accepted. I also realized how many people were open to hearing about clergy sexual assault and had legitimate and thought-provoking questions.

At the same time as I began talking to the media, I began taking social work classes at Grand Valley State University. In one of my first assignments, I risked writing briefly about my assault. At home, after turning in the paper, I was terrified the professor might disregard my assault or inform me I was too scarred to be a social worker and was being dismissed from the program. Imagine my surprise when he wrote an encouraging comment in the margin!

His affirmation inspired me to begin studying clergy sexual assault in as many of my classes as possible. Again, I was surprised when both the faculty and the students were open to what I was studying, because my experience talking to most clergy and denominational leaders had led me to believe it was unacceptable to discuss this topic. My professors' and peers' acceptance empowered me to continue to pursue the topic in nearly all my classes. I began researching the history of sexual assault policy, the chronology of clergy sexual assault, and the treatment approaches used for trauma, rape, and depression, as there were no specific treatment approaches documented for sexual assault by a member of the clergy. Among other things, I learned that psychosis can be prompted by trauma and that post-traumatic stress is magnified when one feels unsupported by one's community.

In January 2010, I took my first research class with Dr. Cray Mulder and was given the opportunity to study a subject of my choice for two semesters. I could not believe this good fortune. I chose to research how women heal spiritually after clergy sexual assault. The two-semester research assignment turned into a four-semester thesis project. This book is the end result of that project and the other school assignments I completed while enrolled in the School of Social Work at Grand Valley State University.

I found the most emotionally challenging part of writing this book to be transcribing the interviews[57] with the research participants who had found a supportive clergyperson and a supportive congregation in which to heal. Time after time, I would leave my computer to pace, breathing deeply to calm my racing heart while drying stinging tears from my eyes. In this regard, Janet's interview was the most difficult for me to transcribe. Following is the part with which I struggled the most:

---

[57] For a thorough explanation of how the interviews with the laborers were conducted, please see the appendices.

> This rabbi who has been my mentor for a long time—he's the one who really made me feel "Yes, I'm the victim. No, I didn't do anything wrong. No, I didn't ask for it. And yes, he believed me." And that was my first step toward healing. . . .So, he was probably the most important person that I was led to that helped me to heal. It was as if I was groping for help. My eyes were closed and my hands were up and I was saying, "Please, help me do something because I'm drowning." And the life preserver was placed in my hands and G-d said, "Okay, grab hold and we'll pull you in." So that was another of those situations which really made me feel that G-d was there.

As I worked with this paragraph, I became jealous of Janet, angry, and overwhelmed with thoughts of "Why her and not me?"

My heart raced. My palms sweated. I stopped typing. My eyes burned with tears. My breathing became shallow and rapid. "Why did *I* have to lose my career?"

I got up and paced.

"Why did *she* find support?"

I paced. I breathed. I paced. I breathed.

"I practically begged clergy to support me and found virtually no concrete support in my community or in the national church!"

I took a deep breath. I paced.

"Why?"

Another deep breath. More pacing.

"Why?"

One more deep breath and my body began to relax. I became calmer and walked back to the computer to continue transcribing Janet's interview.

Shortly thereafter, I typed the paragraph quoted in the script where Janet speaks of the rabbi telling her she had been chosen to be a foot soldier and now she needed to make a decision about what she was going to do. Janet stated that she accepted the draft, and is now fighting the good fight; she fights it every single day.

As I typed this portion of Janet's interview, my heart raced again and my palms sweated. My eyes teared up. I hyperventilated.

I paced. "Why did *she* get called to the battlefield?"

I breathed. I paced.

"Why did *she* find support in her denomination?"

I breathed. I paced.

"I went to four congregations and experienced rejection at all of them!"

I breathed deeply as I paced.

"She wasn't even *looking* for a supportive clergyperson."

Another deep breath. More pacing.

"She didn't lose a career."

More breaths. More pacing.

"Why her? Why not me?"

Another deep breath. My body began relaxing.

"Why?"

And then a still, small voice entered my head: "Because had you found a supportive congregation in your denomination, you would have healed and pursued your career in the church, and then who, *who* would have researched and written this book on healing after clergy sexual assault?"

We may never know why we suffer. But for me, in that instant, the scales that had blinded me as to how Mystery had been at work in my life all along fell from my eyes. I was at peace for the first time in years and felt more connected to both life and Mystery than I ever had. The void and the darkness were gone. They did not return.

As I was nearing the completion of this book, I received a vague phone message from someone who belongs to the congregation where the assault had occurred. I have reestablished some friendships from that congregation and am open to reconnecting with anyone from my past who will acknowledge what my family and I experienced, but this individual was not one with whom I had reconnected. When I received the message requesting my help, my anxiety level skyrocketed and I became nauseous. During the two hours I had to wait before I could return the call, it was difficult to stay present in the moment as my mind raced ahead. What the heck did the caller want? Would I be judged through the conversation? Would I be gossiped about later? My anxiety had less to do with the person who had called and more to do with me and the issues I still needed to work on. I returned the call, only to leave a voicemail. It was another twenty-four hours before I was called back. As I waited, I allowed the situation to control me. I snapped at my husband and children, not knowing why I was angry. Eventually, I recognized my anger as a reaction to the original phone call. In the end, the call was innocent enough. The caller was looking for something and thought I might know its whereabouts.

I share this event because, even though I have come through my dark night to a place of spiritual rebirth, my wound still aches at times, just as a change in the weather causes a throb and a limp in a bone that once was broken. The scar will always be with me; I imagine it will get scratched and will bleed from time to time. My job now is to be aware of when the weather changes and strive not to react too harshly with those I love. Rather than react, I can choose to tend my ache when it throbs and allow it to reconnect me to the overwhelming pain experienced daily by many on this planet. This connection, if I allow it, can become my teacher, reminding me to be present to those who suffer.

Life after clergy sexual assault is dark. The soul can feel as if it has been ripped from the body. But the dark night which follows the assault is an opportunity to know oneself better, to become a more compassionate person, and to become more intimately connected with Mystery. It is my deepest desire for you, if you are a struggling laborer, that by embracing your soul wound and resting in the darkness, you will come to know and express yourself as the beautiful, compassionate person you have been created to be. For, you, too, have been given a trench and have been drafted to the good fight. What are you going to do?

SECTION III:

Voices of Others

Unless someone like you cares a whole awful lot,
nothing is going to get better.
It's not.

—Dr. Seuss in *The Lorax*

Chapter 8

A Husband Remembers

The poetry and soliloquies in this section have been taken from the words of the interviewee. Filler words have been deleted. Words or phrases that have been added are found in [brackets].

The following poem is drawn from an interview with the husband of a laborer who was not one of the eighteen interviewed for this book. He shares his experience and thoughts on the subject.

Living with the Sexual Assault of My Wife

It is so individual.
I don't think I could give advice to other husbands.

It was shocking
when I first had suspicions something was going on.
I remember
seeing her talking to Joe
and
realizing by the way she was talking to him that she was in love with him.
I thought to myself,
"Shit,
she's in love with him!"
Then, a short time later, she came to me
and
told me they were spiritual twins.
At first,
I somewhat bought into it
and

thought,
"Maybe they are."
But there was a lot of resistance to it, too.
It was burdensome.
I didn't know it was abusive at that time.
But
early on in the relationship,
I read some of the emails between her and Joe
and
I realized he was manipulating her by creating this
outlandish story
that she bought into.
I hated him.
This is hard to talk about.

She fell apart for months.
I had to carry everything.
EVERYTHING!
The kids.
The finances.
EVERYTHING!
I eventually filed for divorce because it became too much.
I wasn't going to put up with that shit anymore.
We got a divorce.
It tore our family apart.
I went and bought a separate house.
One of our children was deeply impacted by it
and
went from being a straight-A student,
enthusiastic about things,
to being
a depressed rebel.

I didn't want to be divorced.
Just before we divorced,
their relationship ended.
Then everything exploded about the same time.
We got a divorce.

Then the church found out about the relationship
and
they got rid of him.
I didn't have a problem with that.
But the congregation assumed it was an affair
and
blamed her for it.
And then living in this community
with all those people from the congregation
was awkward.
I stopped going to church,
but it didn't destroy my faith.
It put the nails in the coffin
because
I was already questioning a lot before then.
When all this was going on with the church,
she fell even more apart.
I was hoping she would get better.
I still loved her.
But she was nonfunctional.
Something had to be done.
I didn't want my kids to go through more than they
already had.
Things between my wife and me got a lot better
once Joe was out of the picture.
In the aftermath,
she and I started talking
a lot.
She talked endlessly about the relationship
and
I listened.
We were able to gradually put things back together,
although things will never be the same.
We did marry again.
It was good for our kids that I stuck around
because our kids got to have a home
with both their mom and dad in it.
Our relationship is now good,
but that took some time.

If someone is going through this with their wife,
they have to make a decision.
It might get better,
but
you have to work on yourself
a lot
to accept all the shit
that happened.
If you are not able to come to the point where
you can accept it,
then it is probably better to walk away
because
you are just going to be too pissed to have a good marriage.
I think a lot of people would never be able to accept what had
happened
and
to continue on with their marriage.
For me,
I was able to work through this by turning to Buddhism
and
learning how to meditate
and
learning to accept everything in life as it is
and
that not everything is how you want it to be.
It takes time to come to that point, though.
But
it was worth it.

Today
I feel like my marriage is better in a lot of ways
than it was before.
We do not have illusions like we used to,
the illusions you grow up with
about how things should be,
like illusions about the husband being the
knight in shining armor
and
the wife being the faithful virgin who can do no wrong
or something like that.

(laughs)
We're able to talk honestly
about
everything.

But
I still,
on some level,
blame her for what happened.
On some level,
I think if she didn't want it to happen,
it would not have happened.
I understand it is the pastor's responsibility
and
that he holds all the power
and
is able to manipulate people.
But
as a husband who lived through the nightmare,
I have not been able to completely place all the blame on Joe.
I am no longer angry about it.
It is what it is.
It happened.
Nobody's perfect.
I don't know what the statistics are,
but
over half the marriages have infidelity
and
that is the light I see it in to some extent,
even though
it was infidelity caused by
manipulation and abuse,
but
from my perspective,
there was some
infidelity.

I don't really like to talk about this.

Can we talk about something else?

In living through this,
I see healing
in her
because in struggling to deal with this,
she has become a much more independent person.
She doesn't have all the illusions and expectations
that a woman growing up in the church has.
Our kids see life more realistically
than they would if this had not happened.
And for me,
I think having gone through this,
I feel I can handle pretty much anything that life throws at me.
There are very few crises that I can see that would crush me
emotionally or spiritually.
I can only think of one or two that would do that.
So I think that everyone came through this stronger,
although
one of our children still has some struggles
which haven't been dealt with
that stem from this
and
how the church responded.

The church really needs to prepare their pastors much better
if they are going to be counseling people.
They need to actually give them extensive
training in counseling,
rather than think that because they know the Bible
they can counsel,
because
they can't.
They are not qualified.
The church should probably have more oversight over
their pastors
because
this happens all the time.
They should have some sort of unified or common response
to explain to the congregation what happened
so the congregation doesn't just drive out

the
[so-called] evil-doer.

My wife
was treated as
the
evil-doer!

Chapter 9

A Husband's Soliloquy

The following soliloquy is from an interview with Laurie's husband.

My Wife

When the clergy sexual abuse occurred, we weren't married. We met in September 1992, and I don't think I actually knew [about it] until sometime in the spring of the following year, when Laurie actually confided in me. She was involved in talking about it with the church she was currently attending, and she had confided to one of the pastors. He convinced her she was obligated to report it and was leading her through the process. That was all done without me in her life.

In June of 1993, our relationship became more serious. As she so charmingly tells people, "He hired me, then fired me so he could marry me." While we were dating, that is also when we started our negotiations with the insurance company on behalf of the church. So that's really how I became involved, talking with Laurie and helping her decide what was best for her. Did she want this to go to trial? Did she want to sue? When she confided in me and talked to me about what happened, it explained a few things in some of our more intimate times that we had before I actually knew of the clergy abuse. But I don't think there was any flag for me; it just kind of clicked and made sense.

I think the hard part was trying to walk her through all this. Her feelings were starting to bubble up about the loss of her [community] and her church and her ultimate goal and dream to become a pastor in the ELCA. [I had to be] more cautious with her and more understanding.

We got married in '94. I would say until early or middle of '95, there were still a lot of scars that hadn't healed yet, that were open because of her communicating with the bishop of the synod where the abuse took place. When I met her, she was vivacious and youthful and had a million-dollar smile. Once she was confronted [by the bishop and his men] and made to feel like it was her fault and there was no accountability on the pastor, it kind of changed her inside with her God and with the church.

I remember her describing the meeting with the bishop and his group and just how ugly they were in their demeanor and their questions. I would hope they would conduct themselves a little bit better and provide advocates a little better today than they did back then, being that that was almost twenty years ago.

But I think at that time, the [offending] pastor seemed to be the bishop's chosen child and was really well liked by the ELCA. In my opinion, they wanted to try and pin this on Laurie as being her fault and not this guy [failing to abide] in his oath as pastor and his commitment to God.

But to me, it was very frustrating and made me angry because here was a person who really affected her life and her intimacy, as well as her trust. I think that it still, even to this day, has a little bit of an effect on us because there are times when something is bothering her and she is not willing to bring it up and talk it through. I don't know if it's directly related, but at times she says, "So-and-so [from the congregation's] daughter is doing this," or "I heard from somebody from [my former community]." There are those fond memories that she would like to have, but all they do is bring up this really horrible experience she had to go through that affected her life negatively.

And this guy got put on a shelf and brought back out and there is no accountability. And that still angers me to this day, that he would be allowed to go back into ministry, because I think that doesn't show the validity of what Laurie went through. Then she signs this [silencing agreement] and it's really not [the ELCA's] concern anymore. One of the things we kept trying to stress is that we said we didn't think this guy should be a pastor again. We didn't think this guy should be put back in a church and trusted to lead a church family.

I don't know what counseling the church put him through, but I do know that the bishop was never one to follow up. It was kind of like, "Laurie did this and now we don't want anything to do with you." No one ever called to check up on Laurie or to see how she was. It was like, "We handed you your money, now go away. That's all you wanted."

And that's not really what the issue was. I think Laurie would [have *not*] taken any money [if it would have ensured] he was not a preacher again. They brought in one guy to talk to us. Then they brought in another guy. I had a couple of phone calls and they put an offer on the table and said, "That is it. Either take it or we go to court."

I talked to Laurie; we consulted lawyers, and decided to take the offer. She needed to sign the boilerplate disclaimer. In the disclaimer it was stated that she couldn't talk about it and she couldn't come back later and inform the church or inform anybody that it happened in his past history.

I think that it tainted me from the very beginning. I didn't want to be involved in anything with the ELCA. For the first ten years of our marriage, we never joined a church. We were very mobile in those first years due to the work I do, and that was part of it. We always found a way to be involved in church—service and worship. We attended but did not join. In our current city, we found a church we really liked, but when we got into it, I felt the church was really an instrument of the bishop and it wasn't really its own congregation. We didn't need that again. The church that we now attend is no longer in the ELCA but is in the North American Lutheran Church. That is a better community for us to be involved with by far.

Laurie's in the room now and we might get into an argument [about my saying this] when we hang up, but I think she is still angry at God, that God would let this happen when a pastor is what she believed she was created to be. And I think that has deeply scarred her and has made her feel worthless at times in her life. She was so focused on what her dream was and so close to achieving it, and then because somebody was irresponsible and didn't live up to his commitments and his oath, she had all that tossed away.

When she gets down, I remind her we have had twenty great years together. Currently, we live in a lovely home, and where we live is a beautiful place, but there is still that empty part of her that will never be filled until she ministers again. She always has [ministered], to some extent. That never stopped. It couldn't. It's who she is. But the path to seminary was halted. And for that I feel horrible for her.

As a person who works with a lot of young people, I am around college students every day. There is a great sense of responsibility that I have mentoring these youth. Probably now being older, being fifty and understanding how an older man might think about how a twenty-one-year-old might look more attractive . . . but to do what that pastor did—it's the worst of the worst. Not only is it like rape, but it is a person of God who you expect to fulfill his covenant and responsibilities and keep you safe and protect you. Then I look at it and say that she got cheated out of something in life [that] she wanted. When I think about it personally and professionally, I don't ever want to ruin my relationship of trying to help and nurture and coach these young people and then have them turn around and say, "Well, he is just a pervert!" I can only imagine the destruction that would cause. My morals and ethics keep me from doing it.

But I look at someone like that pastor and say, "How could you do that? How could you let that person down?" [That's true of] everybody who crosses that line. I think that's the norm in America right now—if you cheat a few times, or you tell a lie or two, or if you kind of slip down that moral or ethical road, it's [seen as] okay. I mean, we all sin—I know that. But I just think it's so important to keep that honesty, that integrity, that trust.

I look at it more as I'm very lucky. I have a smart wife, a beautiful wife. A wife who is an intellectual, politically and sports minded, and deeply connected with God.

When I look back at that time [before we met], I wanted somebody I could take care of. I wanted somebody that I could build a great life with. I think a lot of our beginning relationship, the first five or maybe ten years, I took care of everything—the cooking, shopping, cleaning. I don't want to sound like Laurie couldn't do anything, but I was trying to take as much of the burden off her life and kind of put it on me to say, "Let me take care of that." Our relationship has grown and matured, and God is good. She is letting some things go, but I still want to make sure that I'm not handing her too much. But

I think in the very beginning, I was trying to do all that so she could heal.

As for me, I will say that a unique experience at our NALC church was when the congregation was going through our final vote to leave the ELCA and the bishop didn't show up but a representative of the bishop did. I really bit my lip a couple of times because I wanted to lay into this woman about what the ELCA did to Laurie. I didn't. I have more self-control than that and am more disciplined as a person than that. I think they knew the writing was on the wall regarding our congregation's vote, and they sent a mope. This wasn't the bishop or an assistant to the bishop. It was like they thought, "They are leaving anyway," so they sent the mope. So, I didn't bother the mope.

Throughout all this, my relationship with God remained strong. In my mind, my role was to try and help Laurie get through this. From my perspective, I don't think I've done as good a job as I could have because it didn't happen to me, and I don't really fully understand her frustration with God and with the church. I felt it was my job at times to be the leader in that role. One of the things that was very attractive to me about Laurie was her faith in God; she knew the Bible very well and she was, and is still to this day, very good with prayer.

I'll end with this: A pastor friend of Laurie's for decades immediately came to her defense by calling her abuser "a predator." He also stressed that praying together is one of the most intimate things a couple can do together, and we can attest to that. We have much to thank God for through all this.

Chapter 10

A Mother Remembers

The following poem reflects the experience of a mother enduring the pain of her daughter's assault.

My Daughter

What is it like for a mother
to watch her adult daughter
descend into hell,
into the darkness that results
from clergy sexual assault?

My fears began as my husband and I
were traveling and my cell phone rang.
It was my daughter.
Immediately,
she told me
about a vision she'd had.
I said,
"You mean you had a dream?"

"No.
It was a vision.
I was wide awake."

I'm not used to such talk.

In my world,
having a concrete vision is not normal.
A
big
knot of fear
enveloped me.

In her vision,
a man came into her living room
and
raped her.
She said
it was so vivid
it was as if it was
actually happening.

As if that
wasn't frightening enough,
when I asked
who the man in her vision was,
she said,
"Satan."

"Satan!"
I exclaimed,
horrified.
"What does that mean?"

She ignored
my question,
continuing,

"I
was scared,
but
then I looked and saw
Jesus
standing behind the couch,
reassuring me.
He was smiling
and said,
'It's okay.
Everything will be okay.'"

BUT IT WASN'T OKAY!
I just didn't understand
how terribly wrong
it all was.

How can it ever
be okay
to be raped,
whether it's
figuratively,
spiritually,
emotionally,
mentally,
or
physically?

Why would
Jesus
be standing there saying
it was okay?

What in the world had prompted
such a terrible vision?
And what did it mean?
When I asked
what she thought it meant,
she said
dully,
"It doesn't matter."

I told her
a hallucination
could be the sign
of a chemical imbalance
in the brain,
that she should go
to a doctor
because
they had medicine for this.
She said that
medicine
couldn't help
what was wrong
with her.

Then
she told me
about other strange
spiritual
visions
and
spiritual
coincidences

that
she and Pastor Joe
had experienced.
I was greatly troubled
by what she said,
but
at this point
I still trusted
her pastor.
Even so,
I was alarmed by the whole
far-out
conversation.
As she talked,
I had a vague feeling
that in some
remote way,
she was
calling out
for help,
but
I didn't
know how
to help.
I didn't know
[that] the root of her problem
was that she was being sexually abused by
Pastor Joe.
She wouldn't say that.
Unbeknownst to me,
Joe had insisted on,
had sworn her

to secrecy—
a typical ploy of
clergy abusers.
That night
was the first night
of many nights
I cried myself to sleep.

"What's wrong with her?"

I knew
the dream/vision/nightmare
spoke
volumes,
that it had
many layers of meaning.
But
exactly
what it meant
I would never have imagined
in a million years!
I was
totally ignorant
on the issue
of clergy sexual misconduct [against] adults
and
the internal violence,
spiritual devastation,
and
psychological trauma

done to women
by such
an assault.
Research shows
that trauma
can cause
psychosis.
So
my first fear
that my daughter was suffering
from
a mental-health condition
was right.

I had watched
my daughter grow
from childhood
into a
giving,
balanced,
well-educated
young
woman of faith.
I saw
that change
dramatically
as she
began
to crumble
before my eyes
and
descend

into a pit of darkness.
That's the only way I can describe it.
My daughter
was becoming
a stranger,
wandering restlessly
in a strange land.
It wasn't
where she belonged,
and
it caused
all sorts of
upheavals.
Much later I read
[that] this is normal
for women
in this situation.
It's as if they are in
a war zone.

I eventually
came to feel
as if she were
in an invisible prison
and
Pastor Joe
had gained too much power over her thinking.
We all stood by,
bewildered,
wondering
what was happening
to her.

She often had a spaced-out,
haunted look
in her eyes,
as if she were possessed
by some other entity.
In social settings,
she seemed to be unable
to concentrate.
She'd sit
among us
as if she were

far,

far

a
w
a
y
.

At such times,
her mind seemed
vacant of thought.
She seemed
to withdraw inward
to
a secret,
safe
place
where

nothing could hurt her.
She became
unable
to do
basic housework.
She had wildly
contrasting moods,
from fetal positions
on the couch
for hours
as she seemed
to cower
in fear,
to a lack
of her usual morals
in many areas.
She seemed
childlike one moment,
a free spirit the next,
a forlorn refugee another time.

At one point,
handfuls
of
her thick hair
started
falling out,
signs of
the great
internal
stress
she was under.

She had put up
a wall
around herself
and
we weren't able
to get in
to help
her.

I only saw Joe once
during that time.
It was in her driveway.
He drove by,
saw me,
and
stopped.
Before I had a chance
to question him,
she came walking up the driveway
with a knit cap pulled down over her ears.
It wasn't even cold out.
It was the middle of summer!
As she approached us
and
began talking with Joe,
she became like
an
acquiescent
little
girl
in a trance.

I wanted to reach over,
shake her,
and scream,
"What's the matter with you?"
But
I couldn't because
she was
too
fragile
emotionally.
I was afraid
she might fracture
into a million pieces
and
she'd never be able
to be made whole again.
As I watched this interaction,
I began to see
the relationship
in a new way,
as a two-person cult.
She had developed
the typical mindset of a
cult member.

As
I reflect back
on that
torturous time,
of watching
the kaleidoscopic changes
in her,

I realize how
all of us in her family
were living in
a distorted reality.
I constantly felt
as if we were
in a surreal world
where it was hard for any of us
to find firm footing
as the ground
kept convulsing
under us.
Our ability
to act decisively
—or at all—
regarding the situation
became strangely frozen
as we navigated
through
confusing
tunnels
of
endless

c
. i
s r
e c
l

Our sense of being
seemed suspended

in a bizarre world
of distorted illusion
and
inward pain.

Because of the freezing
of our ability
to think
or act
normally,
it took a long time
for us
to put the pieces
of the puzzle
together
into a realization
of the appalling truth
of what had actually happened
to our daughter.

If the church
educated their people
on this issue
like they definitely should,
there would be less sexual abuse by clergy,
more awareness by family when it happens to a loved one,
and
by church members when it happens in their church.
This would create more embracing and healing for victims.

So why does the church so adamantly refuse to address this
issue in a Christian manner?

After disclosure was made in my daughter's church,
many in her church "family,"
as well as bishops, pastors, and other leaders,
deserted her,
judged her,
shunned her,
and
sought to silence her,
even as they smiled with false sympathy,
pretending they cared.
As I listened to the anemic bishops
and
watched their calculated moves,
I wept.

If the church had resolved this situation
with true justice,
then my daughter
(and other victims)
wouldn't have been kept
in hell
for so many additional years
after the abuse had stopped,
and
the rest of us
wouldn't have
had to watch
as her congregation,
various church leaders,

and pastors
revictimized her
and put the final nails
into her spiritual faith.
I'm tired of the lies told by my church,
disillusioned by the cold-heartedness
of pastors and leaders.
I once loved my church.
They helped instill in me a love for justice
through their teachings,
yet refused that same justice
to my daughter
and other victims.
I always believed
their liberal stance on issues
made them more compassionate.
I was wrong.

I thought they truly represented
the teachings of Jesus.
Again,
I was wrong.

It wasn't Jesus' words about
justice and mercy,
but rather secular law,
that determined
how little they were required to do
in helping victims of clergy sexual abuse.
They refused to go beyond
the letter of the law

into the all-inclusive world
of God's grace.

All of this hasn't affected my faith in Jesus as Lord of my life,
but
I no longer look at the institution of the church with adoring eyes.
I still worship God on Sundays,
as the Spirit moves me,
but
the church is constantly in need of reformation,
of reforming it into what it was meant to be.
I know it will never be perfect,
but it must learn to be just
and embrace the broken ones of this world.
If I didn't believe we could reform the church,
I wouldn't have been willing to share the pain
our family went through.
The more we break the silence
and
share the truth when we see the church is oppressing others,
the more we will bring change to the church.

Break the silence.
Heal the pain.
Stop clergy abuse.
Stop blaming victims.

Chapter 11

A Grandmother Speaks

The same woman whose words are shared in chapter 10 also addressed how her daughter's sexual assault impacted her grandchildren.

My Three Grandchildren

I'm growing older,
my hair is gray,
and
my step is slower
than
it was when
my first grandchild was born
over nineteen years ago.
As the years passed,
my daughter
gave me
two more
beloved grandchildren.

I have lived my life for Jesus,
teaching Bible studies
and
worshipping regularly.
I was overjoyed

to know that all my children and grandchildren
were also
very involved in the church.
The world
outside
is full of
danger
and
harm.
Here
inside this sacred place
I thought
they were safe.

Ah!!
How little I knew.

I've watched three children's deep and innocent faith

s
l
o
w
l
y

die
as, one by one,
bishops,
pastors,
and
many in their church family

judged,

gossiped,

ignored,

rejected,

and

CONDEMNED

their mother,

traumatizing

my grandchildren

into realizing that many of those who follow Jesus

didn't really believe any of the stuff they preached,

such as

love,

forgiveness,

reconciliation,

and

mercy.

And

in their

pain and hurt,

their faith

died.

I sat in horror at this evil,

and

I

cried.

I cried

because of leaders who didn't educate congregations
on the
trauma, devastation, and dynamics of clergy sexual abuse.

I cried
for the judgmental people in congregations
who
didn't even realize what they were doing.

And
I cried
for
all the spiritually broken children of abused women.

Children
seem to be
the forgotten victims.

Yet
there is no doubt
that the sons and daughters
of abused women
have been through
their own
hell
and
their own
trauma
at the hands
of the church.

I have pictures

of my grandchildren
at the altar
receiving their First Communion,
believing . . . .

But
for these same grandchildren,
there will never be
a picture
remembering
the joys of
a Confirmation Day

because
the church
forgot
to remember
my grandchildren.

Why
did they
forget
my grandchildren?

Chapter 12

A Minister's Soliloquy

After her assault, Nancy sought the support of a minister outside her denomination. When she and I had finished her interview, she asked if I would be interested in talking with him. Of course, I agreed.

It Was Just Horrible

Nancy came into my office. I think she called up and said, "Hey, do you have time? I need to talk?"

She came in. We were in my office. I said, "Feel free to sit down."

She said, "No, I think I want to stand."

Which was fine, but as she was telling me that she was a victim of clergy abuse and Joe told her if she really had to talk to somebody, it might as well be me because I seemed like a good guy, I thought, "What the hell does that mean? Did he think that I would help to hide it, or cover it up, or calm her down, or what?"

But the other thing I remember from that is trying to find some way of referring to it so there wasn't any judgment or stuff like that or gratuitous language. I used the word "affair" and she said, "No, no, no! 'Affair' is romantic and loving. That is not what this was at all!"

Ugggh! I knew that. It was just; there was no good word for it. Nancy just sort of let me learn that and didn't hold it against me. We just kept right on going.

As she was telling me about it, I was thinking, "There is no class on this." At that point I was on my denomination's committee that deals with ministerial standing. I hadn't been on it long, but long enough to realize that this was a real problem and that it really needed to be dealt with by her denomination. So I said, "I can support you. But you are going to need to report this to the Lutherans."

At that point she was just sort of done in. Very high-strung. Emotional. I eventually convinced her that was what needed to be done. And she said, "The interim pastor at my church is the bishop's representative."

I thought, "That would be perfect!"

And she went off to report it to the bishop's representative. I walked down to my secretary, and because Nancy had come from the other direction, she didn't necessarily get seen by the secretary. But there is a mirror outside my office that allows her to see who comes into my office and [the secretary] is pretty savvy. And I said, "Hey, did you happen to notice what time a person came and talked to me?"

She said, "Yeah, I know about what time."

I said, "Would you note that time and this time." Because even though I was absolutely willing and able to believe Nancy, all I really knew was that something was terribly wrong somewhere. And I thought, "Let's just keep a paper trail going."

That afternoon [Nancy] called me back at home, and I can't believe she managed to do this because she had called up the interim minister, the bishop's rep, and he had said, "Well, you know, you need a lot of encouragement and support, and I am sure that's how this got started. Best move on now for everybody."

And my eyes were wide and my jaw was slack and I'm thinking, "What the hell kind of thing is that to say? Has he not read anything? Has he not heard? How do you be the bishop's representative and give that sort of bullshit answer or response or pat on the back or 'Now, now, dear, boys will be boys'?" It was just hideous!

And the fact that she could then call up another male minister and say, "Gosh, I've just been abused again," was just phenomenal to me.

So I don't remember exactly what we did at that point, but I think we went directly to the bishop, and that bonehead would listen and listen and say, "What do you want us to do?"

Which is just a great way of saying, "We really don't want to do anything but we really don't want to have a problem. So tell us what we need to do [to not] have a problem and we'll see if we can do that, so we don't have a problem."

It was just so completely different from [my denomination's] system, which we probably had developed from our own missteps and mistakes and idiocies. But Joe, at the time, was saying that maybe he would just resign his standing. [In my denomination,] a committee did not have to receive anyone's resignation if they were resigning to avoid this sort of charge and conflict. We say, "No, we do not accept your resignation, and we're bringing you up on charges."

The reason for this is twofold. The first [reason] is that a minister who resigns can then ask to be reinstated, and if there is an insufficient paper trail or he goes to another association or committee, he might be able to get reinstated because there is no charge on his record. The other reason is that the denomination can then charge him and make it very clear to him and everybody that this is stupid, wrong, gross, unethical, immoral, and just incredibly destructive.

And one of the things that was clear to me was just how destructive this was to Nancy, for Nancy's family, for Nancy's circle of friends, for Nancy's worshipping community, for Nancy's relationship with the church, for Nancy's relationship with God, for her sense of call in ministry, [her relationship] with her husband, and her trust in the church.

When people are involved in anything that really hurts them, usually they have someplace left [to turn for support], at least the church or at least God. But this just wiped out everything. Every form of support. Everything. It was just a nuclear devastation. It was horrible to watch.

One night she called up and said, "Hey, I've just taken all my Tylenol. I've taken all my antidepressants. I should probably go to the hospital."

And I was thinking, "Yeah."

And at that point, all I had was her side of the story and I'd been burned enough that I'd listened to someone and absolutely believed them, but [until the story is confirmed], I don't act. I hear it as a provisional truth that I receive. So not *really* knowing what I was walking into, I quickly brought my wife, who is also a member of the clergy, up to speed and we went over there. It took the two of us.

That night in the emergency room with her husband, I was able to say, "Is it true that Joe called you up and apologized to you and not to her?"

And he said, "Yes."

At that point, I finally had some kind of independent confirmation of what was going on. But it was really horrible to watch, and I tried to support and tried to take care and tried to protect and reassure her when and if that was needed.

I really, really had to hand it to the Lutherans for finding an unbelievable [amount] of ongoing ways to continue to hurt Nancy in the years that followed. [For example,] they asked Joe to do music for some women's event. It was just incredible.

Just utterly incredible. There is just some point where you have to say, "You don't ask someone who has been sexually inappropriate to lead a women's event in music and call him a minister of music."

I mean, really! That's just in poor taste, and not just for Nancy. What if at that point she decided to have that lawsuit and it came out that the bishop knew about Nancy's abuse for several years? Then all the women there are thinking, "Eww, really? I thought I liked this music. I thought he did a nice job." And all of a sudden all of those women are going to be bruised by it, at least distantly bruised. I mean, use an ounce of brain!

No matter how much I wanted to say, "We're all trying to figure this out," it just seemed like they weren't trying to figure it out. They had read nothing.

Oh, and then when the bishop posts the new minister, he doesn't tell the new minister any history around [Nancy's abuse]. I was thinking, "Oh, come on!"

Nancy went and told the new minister because she just eventually figured out that he had no idea. Nancy should not have been in that position. And the new minister should have known before coming in what he was coming into. That way he could have figured out if he had the wisdom, skill, and interest in dealing with it. He could have been prepared.

At the point that [the new minister] heard [about Nancy's abuse], he said to me, "What this tells me is that I am going to be a long-term interim [rather than a regularly called pastor]. I won't be able to survive very long because of the internal dynamics around this. I sensed something was wrong. Something was amiss. Something wasn't really quite right, but I couldn't put my finger on it."

Secret-keeping is really strong in any church. And so here is another guy who gets some of the shrapnel damage from the whole thing—he and his family. The amount of devastation Joe caused is just incredible. And then for the denomination not to really be able to provide any care or help or anything.

I'm not the one to try to find some soft way of dealing with ministers who do this sort of thing, even if it is not sexual misconduct, because it is just utterly devastating to churches and families, to those that were baptized by him, to those that were married by him, or whatever. It's just horrible. How is that for a sum-up statement? It's just horrible!

Well, Nancy pretty much was a bull in full stride most of the time. A lot of what I did was to keep saying, "Yeah, the bishop is being a bonehead, but you've got a lawyer. Let the lawyer talk to him."

[I was] just trying to let her know that this experience was not the whole of church experience. I was trying to distance the church from God so that she would at least hopefully have God eventually again. I took a great deal of satisfaction that she was eventually able to move again into the church community where I was serving. She would occasionally come and worship, off in the back of the congregation. She actually joined, and I was thrilled that we could get her to that point. Only to have the interim minister in [the congregation I was serving commit sexual misconduct with another parishioner].

My wife and I were associate ministers there. When the senior minister retired, we got an interim minister. About a year and a half after we got the interim, it was clear that he was having an inappropriate relationship with a parishioner. All of a sudden, I had to deal with that right in my own congregation. That week, [my wife and I] went to the church lawyer and said, "There is every reason to believe he is [sexually abusing a parishioner], and these are the reasons we believe it."

The lawyer said, "Unless he resigns, we are going to have to pursue this."

I said, "You can do all of that for the church, but the conference is going to be pursuing this no matter what. They are already on the job. They were my first call." So the next night the abusive pastor resigned [from the church]. My wife and I, as the remaining ministers, sent out a letter to the church.

One of the most painful things I had to do was go and tell the retired minister about what had happened. He just loved the church, and I knew he would be hearing about this. Then I had to go and tell Nancy. Once again, she was beginning to trust and settle in. This was just devastating. Once again, another church, all of a sudden, did not prove to be as safe as she had thought or trusted or hoped or believed. There was nothing I could do to convincingly say, "Yeah, we're still trustworthy."

I pretty much wanted to go and do something myself. It was pretty devastating all the way around, but having to tell Nancy and sit with her—that was just really miserable.

I remember telling the lawyer why I felt our church was responsible and [that] we needed to give some money [to the victim] for therapy. He said, "No. No, don't do that because we have responsibilities. We might be at fault, and admitting responsibility could lead to lawsuits. If you admit any responsibility, it is very hard to counteract."

The lawyer was a church member. He was a good church member and a good lawyer. From the lawyer's perspective, he was dead-on right. You just don't admit things, ever. But that's law. I'm church. If need be, I could always fall back on “I speak *to* the church, not *for* the church,” and “Just because *I* said this doesn’t mean that the *church* said this.” I can do my weasel parsing of words and sentences, too. I mean, what the hell!

So I said to the lawyer, “Okay, fine.” I didn’t agree with him. I didn’t say I was going to do it, and indeed I did pay for a couple of sessions of therapy. I just decided that if it goes to slime, it goes to slime, but this was the right thing to do.

I managed to learn a lot. I learned just how devastating it was. I learned yet again that this sort of clergy malpractice or abuse, it just can’t happen. It is just too devastating all the way around. There is just no good that can come of it.

Some of this is also a matter of time. The Catholics look really bad right now because they are two decades behind the curve. The Lutherans during the time of Nancy’s abuse looked bad because they were maybe a decade behind the curve. My denomination, the United Church of Christ, we probably looked better on occasion because we were right there on the bubble of the curve, as a general rule, which isn’t to say there weren’t or aren’t committees or conferences who didn’t get the memo. I know full well that our denomination had ministers who were unworthy of being ministers and we would move them from one place to another place, two hundred, one hundred years ago, absolutely. I think even into the fifties, the sixties, maybe even into the seventies. I think all the denominations have mishandled clergy abuse, and the lucky ones have just figured it out before the unlucky ones.

When the church [I was serving] had to confront [the interim’s clergy abuse], there were some parishioners who just really wanted to move along. “Move along. Least said, sooner forgotten” was one phrase I heard.

And I said to the moderator who was sent to help the church, "That is not my experience. Whatever you need to do to help the church as the moderator, do [that], but that's not where I'm at, and I do not guarantee that is where I will be at. Yes, a lot of ministry needs to be done, but by no means am I going to soft-sell what happened and why all of this is happening."

And we just agreed to disagree. It wasn't the first or the last time. I also had to protect the woman involved because she was a parishioner, and I knew she didn't want to talk to me in the least, so I had a colleague in another town call her. I forget if they talked or if she just left a message that said, "Look, if you feel like you need a minister to talk to, I am available and willing and able."

The parishioner never did call. Eventually, though, she and I were able to have a talk. At first she tried to blame my wife and me for the whole thing. But then she and I were able to talk about forgiveness, and I was able to say, "You have nothing to forgive. And I have nothing to forgive from you or about you. This isn't yours. The abusive minister should have said, 'NO! And no, and no, and no way!' You may have been willing and interested and all of that, and understandably so, but that just doesn't matter. No. It just doesn't matter!"

Eeeeewww! It's just horrible. (*Laughs.*) That will be my summary statement. It's just horrible. Well, it really is. Too bad I can't find some other more profound way to say it.

Oh, you know, one of the other mistakes I made. Nancy called one night and said, "I want to share a few books about all of this with you."

And I said, "Come on by right now. It sounds like you're heading out, and why not stop by the house and drop them off."

I hung up the phone and I thought, "Sweet Jesus, I just asked her to my home and she has no idea if anybody else is home."

Oh, my God, how did she manage to trust me on that? So I immediately went around and turned on all the lights in the house I could find to turn on. I forget who was there, but I said, "I'm turning your music up loud," so she would know someone else was here.

I thought, "How did I do that?"

But when she got to my house, I apologized and I said, "Nancy, your strength is just phenomenal."

It hurts me that [many of the women in your research] have not found any clergy support. That I have colleagues like that. There are some really good colleagues in ministry out there, and maybe it takes a Nancy to bull her way forward to find what she needs. She astonishes me with her ability and strength to keep going forward with this. And she even went and talked with the bishop's representative, and for him to say, "Well, dear, you probably caused it because you need reassurance all the time."

It was horrible. And every once in a while, I remember one more thing, and it's like, "Ah, crap!" It does not help my cynicism toward the church either.

And it really hurts that folks [who have been abused] haven't found any clergy support or [have only found] nominal clergy support. It just is horrible. It is just horrific all the way around.

Anything that can be done in the midst of it or after the fact to help, to find some way to have these ministers held accountable, whether it is in the denomination or the legal system or both—that is so much better than the more natural inclination to find a baseball bat and have a short conversation with them.

To sum it all up, it was just horrible. It is just horrible.

Chapter 13

A Voice from the Congregation

This chapter is based on an interview with a hospital chaplain who attended a nondenominational church where the pastor engaged in inappropriate sexual relationships with his congregants. Here, she discusses belonging to a congregation impacted by such clergy behavior.

The Ripple Effect

He was always very friendly,
talking to a lot of people,
very engaging.
He worked closely with the leaders that were over certain
ministries in the church.
He was very keen on mentoring them for leadership.
I was a leader over a magazine we were producing
in the church.
I would work late nights.
And the way it happened was,
one night,
I was working late.
He came up behind me
and
kissed me
on the cheek or neck somewhere.
It was very wrong.
It was very uncomfortable.

After it happened,
I went after him and said,
"I think that was very inappropriate."
And he told me,
"I didn't mean anything by it.
You know, you are doing a good job,
and
I just wanted to commend you on the work you are doing."
And then
he
just
walked
away.
I immediately started to question whether I was wrong
or
reading more into it.
I wasn't so sure.
After that,
he,
who had been very friendly,
had always spoken to me,
and
complimented me,
stopped saying anything.

So I felt slightly punished by his lack of attention,
approval,
and
compliments.
He'd walk by
and
not say a thing.

That went on for an extended period of time,
for months,
where it was really noticeable.
Eventually,
I had returned back to his graces
and
he began speaking to me.
But
I do remember
that stark difference in the way he acted towards me.
Our relationship did change after that.
I should have appreciated the change.

Later,
I was really shocked
when I heard what the minister was doing with women
in the church.
But
then it brought me back to my experience.
It validated what I had called wrong.
So, all that I had been thinking,
reframing,
and
trying to make meaning of—
by knowing what he did to other women,
assured me I was on target.
It saddened me.
Knowing what he did catapulted [me into] a type of grief
because
I knew, whoever was found in these situations with him,
that he had pursued them
like a predator.

They were definitely victimized.
My antennae were sharpened.
It hit me pretty hard, in the sense
that what I had experienced was definitely a pattern for him.
It made me mad that he [had] made me feel like it was my fault,
that it was me that was making more out of it.
That angered me
because of all the mental gymnastics
and
anxiety it caused me.
It made me angry because of my vulnerability.
I began to think about how much trust I had put in him,
how much of a pedestal I had him on,
how powerless I felt to really do anything
or
challenge him about it.
It made me feel bad about the church itself and how it was structured.
I really don't think anyone in that structure
felt they had a lot of strength to do anything about it,
primarily because of our theology.
People wouldn't talk,
even if they knew exactly what was going on,
about a particular situation.
They really didn't believe it was the right thing to do spiritually,
to talk about the man of God,
the pastor of the church,
because of
his role and his authority.

They didn't feel comfortable voicing their feelings about it.
Because of the secrecy in the church,
the pastor had numerous relationships.
Later, when I found out about certain women
that were victimized,
I realized
we had believed they just decided to leave the church.
They had just left the church.

Because we didn't know the circumstances of
what was going on,
we felt they had
left the call of God
or
left the will of God for their lives
because
we thought
or
were taught
that if you were called to be in this church,
or
if God led you to this church,
then this was definitely where you were supposed to be—
where God spoke to you,
built you up,
and
blessed you.
This is the kind of teaching we got around spirituality,
so if anybody left,
of course we didn't understand that they were victimized
by the pastor.
We felt that they were just falling by the wayside spiritually.

We felt they had forsaken God,
the church,
and
what it was they were called to do.

People in the church are not really equipped to judge
honestly or truthfully
what is going on.
It is out of the church's ignorance that women are ostracized
in their communities
because
most of the time people don't have a sense of what's true.
That was the case in this church.
Placing the man of God,
or the clergy,
on a pedestal,
the people in the church still believed the voice
of this pastor over the victims.
The hierarchy of his voice,
his needs,
came before the needs of the congregation.
That is unfortunate,
but
the church is structured so this happens.
When people would leave the church,
it wasn't about trying to talk to them and find out what
was going on.
It was hearing what the pastor said about them leaving.
He would preach sermons and mention
the absurdity,
the wrongness,
of people leaving

and
forsaking the call of God on their lives.
I can remember him very clearly preaching
about Jezebel
and
women who would come to the church with the sole intention
of seducing the pastor,
trying to bring him down from
his calling,
his authority,
and
his position.
I could recall him preaching on adultery and the
sin of sexual sins.

Behind the scenes, these were *his* big issues.
I can see that clearly now.

When this gets coupled with your spirituality and how
you've been trained up,
it is very difficult to be clear about how you need
to think about things.
Unfortunately,
that results in a lot of people feeling very ostracized.
If a [woman] was [victimized] and needed someone to talk to,
the church people would be the last people she should talk to,
because the church people are still drinking from the water.
They are still in
the mud,
muck,
and
mire

of that confusion.
This renders the church people
as the last people
you would go to if you were
in this situation
and
in need.

I didn't realize the number of women he victimized was so high.
I still don't have a grasp of how many people.
I just know that the time frame was over ten years.
Surprisingly,
when I talk to people from this church,
I learn about other women.
An old friend that I hadn't seen in over ten years
shared with me
about another woman in this situation with him.
For me,
this speaks to how broad the impact has been after all these years.
It also speaks to the fact that in spite of the secrets that people felt the need to keep,
they still need to talk about it at some point.
I recently came across a friend
and
reconnected with him.
In that conversation,
I also learned about
another woman in this situation with the pastor.

When I learned what the pastor had been doing,
I was in seminary studying for my Master of Divinity degree.

I [began] questioning
the role and the authority that pastors have,
how they teach congregations about their authority
as the man of God,
and
how clergy are in these positions and can behave in these
hurtful and victimizing ways.

In seminary,
we had the responsibility of serving in agencies,
and
I worked in a rape and violence agency for men
who had assaulted their wives or children.
The counselors would do group work with the men
and
provide a space for them to talk about what they had done.
Hearing these men talk about their stories
and
their issues with anger and violence
and
sexual assault
opened me up to the needs perpetrators have.
It was eye-opening and difficult to do,
but
I was really glad it was a part of my seminary training
because
it helped me to think about issues in the lives of clergy
that [go unattended].
It is a real problem.
It's unfortunate that we don't give more attention around these
issues in the lives of clergy because
they are people,

with underlying motivations,
interests,
curiosities,
and
needs.
They share the same issues and struggles as people in other professions and careers.
But because they're in this office
there are perceptions deeply rooted in tradition and history
of who they should be,
and
many feel forced to live up to these perceptions
but in reality, they can't.
Where do they have the space to literally live out,
get help,
and
deal with
their issues?
Does the church provide that space for clergy?
I don't think we do.
This could be part of what leads to victimizing behaviors.

We give pastors
a lot of power
and
a lot of authority.
We grant it to them.
I don't think we have a lot of mechanisms or measures
to even question the power they have in congregations.
I'm a chaplain,
but
I am not ordained with a denomination.

And it's hard to explain that to people.
It's a thing where,
"Yes, I know I need to be affiliated here."
But then on the other hand,
it's almost like I feel called to people who have been marginalized
and
are outside of the church.
I am actually in that process now of trying to find my place.
It has been very hard for me to find a church,
be a part of a church,
function in it,
and
even seek pastoral support for myself.
This has slowed down my process,
as far as ordination.
I just haven't found a denomination where I fit well.
But
I am also very keyed in to this issue
of women and children who have been sexually abused
in the church setting or by clergy.
Church should be a safe place.
Most people go to church and treat it as if it is safe,
but
there are many instances
where it is not safe for everybody.
My heart really goes out to doing ministry in this area.
I just haven't quite figured out how to go about it yet.
Maybe my place is not inside the church right now.
Since graduating from seminary,
I keep hearing about cases in the news
where kids or women have been assaulted.

It has been named a lot of different things.
And I'm always wondering:
Where are the women and children spiritually?
Where have they gone?
Are they just out there?
Literally,
just out there?
My heart really breaks about that
because
I know there is healing available for them.
I just want to somehow create a venue for healing,
a place where they can really grow,
tell their stories,
be heard,
find community,
begin to find their voice again,
their place with God,
and
their passion.
A lot of their passion is rooted not only [in] these experiences
but in the things they are destined to do.
I'm sure these women have great contributions to make
in the world,
in their lives,
in their families,
and
with people,
but
sexual abuse and assault have a way of
stifling and holding people down.

Liberation needs to happen.

SECTION IV:

Where Do We Go From Here?

It's every man's business to see justice done.

—Sir Arthur Conan Doyle
The Memoirs of Sherlock Holmes

Chapter 14

Laborers

Spirituality and religion do not easily gel with assault, manipulation, and collusion. This incongruity might cause laborers to question their sanity and feel off kilter as they wrestle to reconcile such contrasting concepts. This chapter emphasizes some of the struggles laborers go through and offers some guidelines for healing. Since not all laborers experience the same struggles, many different healing approaches can be taken, as was demonstrated in chapter 5, "Life-Giving Waters." It is the job of each laborer to discover the healing journey that best fits her needs. If you are a laborer and, while reading this chapter, find that some of it does not apply to your situation, feel free to disregard the paragraph or section. This chapter is designed to supplement chapter 5 by addressing or expanding further on some of the more common healing struggles that presented in the research. It also can be used as a resource toward rebirth.

The Immediate Aftermath

If you are a laborer, it is important to realize that you have done nothing wrong. This is easier said than done, especially if you are being blamed by your church family and spouse or partner. It can take years of work to truly believe you are not to blame. You might not even be aware you still harbor feelings of responsibility until something happens to remind you that you hold such beliefs. Educating yourself about clergy sexual assault and its dynamics is a first step in freeing yourself from guilt and responsibility. The "Recommended Reading" section in the back of this book offers a list of books that have proven helpful to laborers and others in their efforts to understand the dynamics of clergy sexual assault.

After the abusive relationship ends, you might find yourself longing to be back in the relationship with the offending clergyperson. This can happen for a variety of reasons. Perhaps you are or think you are in love with him. Perhaps you miss the feeling of having a special calling from God that the clergyperson told you that you had. Perhaps you miss your congregation or church family. Some laborers seek to protect the offending clergyperson. These are all normal responses.

Many women and children who have been severely abused by a partner or a parent still long to be in relationship with the abuser because even abusive people have some good qualities about them that are missed when the relationship ends, or due to the Stockholm Syndrome, as explained in chapter 7, "My Night Journey." Recognizing that the relationship was abusive could take time and can be a slow and painful process. It might also seem much easier to exonerate the abuser and believe the fault lies with you than to believe that someone who represented God would exploit your vulnerabilities using "God talk," your "sinfulness," and his "sacred position" to do so.

Intense Emotion

As you come to realize the nature of the relationship, you might become enraged and desire revenge. Under your rage lie other emotions, which could include sadness, humiliation, shame, fear, or pain. Experiencing the intensity of these emotions and grappling with them can be frightening, especially if they emerge in public places. It is even possible to become lost in or stuck on one particular emotion. A therapist can help you manage intense emotions and learn to move beyond them.

If you have no health insurance, it might be possible to receive therapy through your county's community mental health agency. You might also ask a therapist if she offers or would consider offering a therapy group. Group therapy will likely be less expensive than individual therapy. Another avenue for the uninsured or underinsured is to work with a spiritual director. Many spiritual directors' fees are based on income, and some certified spiritual directors also hold licensure in a counseling field.

When dealing with intense emotions, it might be helpful to determine what present event triggered the emotion. In determining this, you can then construct a plan for how to respond in the future, should a similar triggering situation occur. For example, perhaps you see someone from your former congregation in public, and the fear of being treated harshly causes you to run out of the store crying. Once you recognize that running into certain people in public can be triggering, you can decide ahead of time how to react to that situation. Perhaps you decide to respond in the future by walking toward the person and being overly friendly, loudly and pleasantly saying, "Well, hello, Mary! It's so nice to see you again." You decide ahead of time whether or not to wait for a response. After such a planned encounter, you might find you relish Mary's response or can congratulate yourself on your boldness. Then, with success under your belt, the next time you encounter someone in the store, the experience becomes a little easier.

It is also important to notice how your body responds to something emotionally triggering. Trauma is stored in the body and is often experienced as a racing pulse, holding one's breath, hyperventilating, sweating, shaking, headache, nausea, or tight muscles. Simply changing your breathing pattern can reduce the intensity of the emotion and the body's reaction. You can learn other techniques as well to help rid your body of the trauma. It is beyond the scope of this book to teach such techniques, but some resources are offered in the "Recommended Reading" section.

Sometimes other people will fail to understand the intensity of your emotions or will misinterpret them altogether. For example, many of the laborers mentioned crying when they were in church. Yasmine said that others in the church thought her tears demonstrated her piety and did not understand that they were related to clergy sexual assault. Their misunderstanding caused her to feel further isolated because she was unable to share her pain.

You might have an episode in public where you lose control of your emotions. Although it can be embarrassing when this happens, try to refrain from berating yourself afterward. You wouldn't berate yourself for sneezing in public, would you? Your emotions are just as natural as sneezing.

Ideas to Help Regulate Your Emotions

The following list of ideas for regulating your emotions is not intended to take the place of a licensed therapist who is trained to help you manage intense feelings. Yet, some laborers have found these suggestions helpful in working with powerful emotions:

- Get your body moving. Walk, run, dance, swim, march in place, chop wood, etc.
- Listen to music that expresses the emotion you are experiencing.[58]
- Sing loudly.
- Hum.
- Lie on the ground.
- Sit under a tree.
- Enjoy something beautiful.
- Clean.
- Write a poem or a story.
- Journal.
- Inhale deeply through your nose for four seconds. Then hold your breath for four seconds. Exhale for four seconds. Hold the exhale for four seconds. Repeat as necessary.
- Massage your ears, face, hands, or feet—or, better yet, get a massage!
- Learn a hands-on healing technique, such as Reiki or Quantum Touch®.[59]
- Place a rubber band around your wrist and snap it when you begin to experience an intense emotion or flashback.
- If you have young children, grandchildren, nieces, nephews, brothers, or sisters, enter into their imaginative world.

---

58 Emilie Autumn, *Opheliac*, The End Records, 2009, compact disc. The first CD in the set contains many songs that relate to sexual crimes and the variety of feelings that are unleashed after one experiences such a crime.

59 See the "Recommended Reading" section in the back of the book for introductory books on energy work.

- If you have a pet, spend some time loving it.
- Do something fun with someone.
- Watch a funny movie.
- Belly laugh.
- Garden.
- Meditate.
- Talk to someone you trust.
- Sketch a mandala,[60] paint a picture, paint a room in your house.
- Keep a list of daily joys and unexpected miracles. Read the list when you feel down.
- Eat healthy, well-balanced meals.
- Perform rituals of liberation, such as creating a liturgy of rebirth; burying something symbolic of the person you once were, then draw an image of who you want to become or of the life you wish to have; burning a letter from the offending clergyperson, or one you write expressing your anger, love, or pain, then scattering the ashes or "planting" them to symbolize the new seeds of life you are sowing.
- Help another person.
- Volunteer.

---

[60] A mandala is an art form found in Buddhism and Hinduism. Carl Jung popularized mandalas in the west by using them in psychotherapy. To sketch a mandala, draw a large circle on a piece of paper and have colored pencils, crayons, or another art medium handy. The circle represents the self. Clear your mind. Choose a color and begin at the center. Do not have a plan for what you want to draw; just allow your hand to use the color until you are ready to choose another one. When the circle is filled, the images contained within portray information about you that is just breaking into consciousness. Mandala sketching helps bring knowledge and feelings to the surface before one is able to articulate them verbally.

- Take up a new hobby you've always wanted to do.
- Spend time in nature.
- Get a new hairstyle.
- Enroll in school or a community education class.
- Allow yourself time to grieve what you have lost.
- Allow yourself to get angry at God.
- Explore the rich diversity of the world's religious and spiritual traditions.
- Celebrate your ability to make dinner if you have not been capable of making dinner since the assault.
- Read books about strong people who have overcome great adversity.
- Create new traditions to fill the time you used to spend with your congregation, such as a family breakfast of Belgian waffles topped with strawberries and whipped cream every Sunday morning, a walk in nature, or a new activity such as community theater or a book group.
- Become present by taking in your surroundings with your five senses. List in your head what you are experiencing: "I am walking in the store. I am in the produce section. I see strawberries are on sale this week. I smell the chicken roasting in the store's rotisserie. I hear children laughing. The air-conditioning is making me cold." Such talk can ground you in the present moment and make overwhelming emotions and unwanted thoughts subside.
- Learn how to work through deep trauma with a therapist, using techniques such as Somatic Experiencing or Eye Movement Desensitization and Reprocessing (EMDR).
- Marvel at the wonders of creation.
- Believe in yourself. You are an amazing person.

- Believe you will make it through these experiences. You will.
- Imagine what life will look like when you are on the other side of this.
- Make a list of goals to accomplish today, in a year, in five years. Take steps toward accomplishing them.
- Read a motivational book. Read another. Read one more.
- Embrace the dark night, make peace with it, and discover the wisdom only the darkness can teach.

Spirituality

It would be wonderful if all laborers could find spiritual nourishment in their religious tradition, but this is not always possible. Some must look outside their tradition for a means of surviving and regaining their spiritual footing. It can be frightening to move toward another tradition. Doing so can create feelings of grief, but sometimes it is the only way to move forward. If you are struggling with leaving your tradition, remember that God is omnipresent and bigger than any one set of beliefs. Some of the laborers in this research found that they were able to connect better with a new tradition, while others who looked beyond their tradition found they connected for a while outside and then gradually shifted back toward the tradition they had left. Use this time to explore your options and try to refrain from putting pressure on yourself to have everything figured out as soon as possible. If you are able to relax in the ambiguity, eventually your path will emerge. Learning to do this is difficult, so try not to berate yourself if you are unable to do so right away.

Advocacy

Many laborers were silenced, first by the abusing clergyperson and then by the collusion which followed. Their stories were not told to the congregation in a way which honored them. In the course of their journey, some laborers began websites and told their stories. These websites can be instruments of healing because they can deliver the truth to the congregation, denomination, and other potential virgins at risk. Websites can connect laborers to others who have experienced clergy sexual assault, helping validate their experiences and pull them out of isolation. And in some cases, such as Sarah's, a denomination may support your advocacy work.

But posting information online also comes with risk. For example, Yasmine's posting of her story online led to intensification of the collusion and shaming she experienced; she even received death threats. Another concern is that laborers' needs are great. Although the sharing of one another's stories may be helpful in that it enables a laborer to feel validated, the sheer volume and intensity of stories a website can generate may be triggering to someone who is working through her own trauma, and may in fact keep the laborer stuck at a certain point in her healing. If you decide to go online, remember that not every person who contacts you may be who they say they are. Use caution and common sense to screen people, refrain from giving too much personal information, and periodically do internet searches of your name or web address to ensure that your information has not ended up on questionable sites.

Suicide

Although many of the laborers in this study mentioned having experienced the desire to commit suicide, they chose not to. Suicide is permanent, and the laborers in this study who were at least several years past their assault had attached some sense of purpose to their life again. If you are a laborer struggling with thoughts of suicide, are you aware that the legacy of suicide can be passed from one generation to the next? Is the inheritance of suicidal tendencies truly what you desire to leave to your children, your grandchildren, your nieces, or your nephews? If you come from a family with a history of suicide, you can make the choice not to pass that heritage on to the next generation. You can choose to be strong and pass on the truth that your family no longer takes such drastic actions.

If you are contemplating suicide and are in the United States, you can seek help at 1-800-273-8255. If you live outside the United States, suicide hotlines in your country can likely be found by typing "suicide help" into an internet search engine. You may be hurting horribly right now, but you are not alone. There is hope. There is always hope, and resources and people are available to help. In the back of this book is a list of "Recommended Reading." It may be helpful to look over the list and chose a book or two.

The struggles mentioned in this chapter can lead to rebirth, but birth is never easy. Sometimes labor slows; sometimes it is intense. Think of the struggles described in this chapter as labor contractions. Allow the contractions of your rebirth to wash over you, realizing you are in the midst of a hallowed process of becoming. To use Juliana's words, "You are in the process of becoming a *more authentic human being*." You can move beyond this trauma to have a fulfilling and rewarding life.

Chapter 15

Family and Friends

After clergy sexual assault, laborers are forever changed and can never go back to who they were before the assault. No longer do they have an innocent view of clergy, God, or the church. They have experienced how God and power can be misused and distorted for personal gain. The soul has been wounded, and laborers need the acceptance and understanding of those who love them.

The most important thing you as a family member or a friend can do for a laborer is to believe her and recognize that she was victimized and the assault was not her fault. Even if what she says sounds outlandish to you, remember that the clergyperson is solely responsible.

The second most important thing that can be done for a laborer is to listen to her story again, and again, and again. Sometimes she may rage through her story. Other times she may weep. But each time she tells her story, it has a healing effect on her and she is able to process another small piece of it.

It can be difficult and overwhelming to listen to her. But try to listen and refrain from talking as much as possible. Sometimes it might be tempting to interrupt and try to make things better because it is painful and uncomfortable to see someone you love in despair. But in order to heal, a laborer needs to be heard and believed, repeatedly. Validate her story, and if she blames herself, reinforce the fact that she was not at fault. Refrain from giving spiritual suggestions, such as she needs to pray or go to church. She may not be able to do those things. She may never be able to do them. Ever. And that's okay.

If your faith is such that you find this troubling, remember that God has been revealed through the world religions as having compassion on the broken-hearted. God loves the laborer more than it is humanly possible to understand. It is okay if she cannot return to the faith of her family. In God's eyes, she is not lost. She is not condemned. She has been abandoned and wounded by the faithful, just as Christ and John of the Cross and others were abandoned and wounded by the faithful. To love her and to be present to her is a holy act.

Some laborers may choose not to share their story with you. If this is the case, refrain from prying. If it needs to come out, it will. In some cases laborers have buried certain aspects of the story only to discover them much later—even years later.

The laborer may have mood swings and lash out angrily at those around her. Don't take this personally, but understand that something may have triggered an aspect of the assault in her. This response should lessen over the course of time and with therapy.

Significant Others

If you are a spouse or a partner of a laborer, you, too, have been traumatized and wronged by the clergyperson. As difficult as it may be, try to refrain from blaming her and from prying into the sexual details if she is not ready to share them. Perhaps your partner believed she was in love with the offender, but in time, it is likely she will recognize how she was manipulated and exploited.

Perhaps your sexual relationship has been impacted by the assault. If you are able to be supportive and compassionate to her, it is possible that your relationship will mature to a much more intimate place as the two of you work through this difficult time. Remember that true intimacy is much more than the sexual act and that eventually, it may be possible to restore sex in the relationship. Sometimes a laborer needs to be held. Other times she may need distance. You may need to ask her permission to hold her because having been sexually violated may make it difficult for her to be touched.

You may find yourself grieving for the relationship you once had or the person your partner once was. Allow yourself time and space to grieve.

Forgiveness

Some laborers' stories may be violent. Some laborers tell stories of being in love with the offending clergyperson. But regardless of the circumstances, the laborer did not sin, nor does she need your forgiveness, though she may ask for it. In such instances, it may be appropriate to assure her that you do not hold her responsible for any wrongdoing.

Above all, do not tell her that God forgives her. To grant her forgiveness or tell her that God forgives her would be as ludicrous as telling someone that God forgives her because a tree fell on her house or forgiving someone because he was stung by a bee.

Likewise, do not tell a laborer she needs to forgive the clergyperson. She may eventually come to a place in her life where she is able to forgive, or she may never come to that place. Frederick Keene, a New Testament scholar, argues that victims of abuse should never be asked to forgive their abuser. He writes about the concept of forgiveness in Christianity and concludes that in the New Testament forgiveness is always granted by equals or by someone in power to someone in a lesser position. For example, we don't forgive those from whom we borrow money. However, those from whom we borrow money may forgive our debt. Likewise, Keene contends that if Jesus had intended the weak to forgive the strong, he himself would have done so when he was being crucified. Instead, the Gospel of Luke records that as Jesus was hanging on the cross, he addressed God, saying, "Father, forgive them, for they know not what they do" (Luke 23:34, KJV).

> This is a situation where Jesus has no power; he is speaking from a cross about those who have crucified him. What is noticeable is that he does not forgive them. Instead, he asks his Father, he asks God, to forgive them. . . . This is the one place where, if Jesus wanted the weak to forgive the strong, he could have indicated it. He did not. He asked the strongest to forgive, and, being the less powerful, did not offer the forgiveness himself.[61]

Encouragement

Rather than encouraging her to forgive the offending clergyperson, you will prove more helpful by encouraging her as she makes decisions in her daily life. After the assault, some laborers are not able to care for their children or do simple daily tasks such as grocery shopping, cooking, or driving a car.

---

[61] Frederick W. Keene, "Structures of Forgiveness in the New Testament," in *Violence against Women and Children: A Christian Theological Sourcebook*, ed. Carol J. Adams and Marie M. Fortune (New York: Continuum, 1995), 128.

They may need to relearn how to order their day. It may feel natural for you to take on the responsibility of making choices for the laborer, but this is not helpful. Encourage her to make her own choices. Suggest she make a daily to-do list, and become her cheerleader. At first, one small task may be all she is capable of doing in a day. Remember how Amy felt that making a to-do list was a major accomplishment? The laborer has a mountain to climb; celebrate each tiny step she makes!

Self-Care

Life after clergy sexual assault can be difficult if you are one of the supportive people in the laborer's life. You may find yourself experiencing some of the same intense emotions as the laborer. You may also find yourself thrown into the midst of your own dark night of the soul. These are normal reactions when someone you love has been abused.

An outside support person can help you process some of this turmoil. Outside support may include a mental health professional, a supportive member of the clergy, a spiritual director, a close friend, or a family member. Exercising and hobbies are helpful means of self-care. Watching a comedy and maintaining a sense of humor are also helpful ways to relieve tension. Remember to take care of yourself. You have needs, too, and are engaged in difficult, but sacred, work.

Chapter 16

Congregations and Denominations

The denomination's and congregation's responses to a laborer are the largest determining factors in her healing. Terence Gorski, an internationally recognized expert on mental health and violence, echoes this when he writes:

> Safe and supportive environments that encourage talking about the trauma in an accepting and non-judgmental atmosphere, and encourage a personal process of recovery, lower the incidence and severity of PTSD. Nonsupportive environments that deny the trauma, minimize its severity, criticize or judge the victim for having symptoms, and fail to encourage a personal recovery process increase the incidence and severity of PTSD.[62]

Because the environment is a crucial variable regarding a laborer's likelihood of developing PTSD, it is imperative that religious organizations change the way they respond to clergy sexual assault. Denominations need to create an atmosphere

---

62 Terence T. Gorski, "PTSD in Children and Adolescents," February 1, 2002. http://www.tgorski.com/terrorism/PTSD%20Children%20& %20Adolescents.htm#Posttraumatic Stress Disorder In Childhood and Adolescence: A Review.

of zero tolerance in regard to such assaults. Policies supporting laborers need to be drafted and followed by denominational leaders. Although some denominations, such as the Evangelical Lutheran Church in America (ELCA), the Unitarian Universalist Association of Congregations, and the United Methodist Church, have prevention and response policies, this research demonstrates that such policies are not always followed.[63] In part, this has to do with the denomination's regional body (synod, district, etc.) and the congregation's autonomy in relation to the national expression of the denomination at which level guidelines or policies are set. But this is not always the case. Furthermore, some denominations and independent congregations, such as the congregation Angela belonged to; don't have any policies or protocols in place for cases of clergy sexual assault or other forms of misconduct.

It is imperative that bishops and other denominational leaders be provided with training in how to work with and support laborers. There is a common belief among religious leaders that those who have been sexually victimized by clergy do not want to hear from religious leaders. The research be-

---

[63] The policies for these three denominations can be found online: Evangelical Lutheran Church in America, *An ELCA Strategy for Responding to Sexual Abuse in the Church* (Chicago: Evangelical Lutheran Church in America) 2005. http://www.elca.org/Growing-In-Faith/Vocation/Rostered-Leadership/Leadership-Support/Safe-Place/General-Resources.aspx; Darryl W. Stevens, ed., *Handling Sexual Misconduct Complaints: A Handbook for United Methodist Bishops and Cabinets* (Chicago: The General Commission on the Status and Role of Women), 2011. http://www.umsexualethics.org/LinkClick.aspx?fileticket=yDFdp1qsZLw%3D&tabid=8591; Unitarian Universalist Association, *Restorative Justice for All: Unitarian Universalists Responding to Clergy Sexual Misconduct* (Boston: Unitarian Universalist Association), 2002. http://www.uua.org/safe/misconduct/restorative/.

hind this book demonstrates that nothing could be further from the truth. Most laborers hunger and thirst to be supported by the leaders in their congregation and denomination, especially after the assault is disclosed. When leaders fail to respond to laborers and cut off contact with them, it contributes to the isolation and shame the laborer feels. It is retraumatizing and is perceived as collusive.

But when leaders earnestly reach out to laborers regardless of the amount of time that has passed, it has a healing effect. Remember the impact such support had on Juliana even years after her assault, when her pastor friend heard her story and, at the risk of losing his job, advocated for changes in the denomination. This incident was so healing to Juliana that she was able to more fully explore her spiritual path and return to work again as a hospital chaplain after nearly six years of not working in the field. Although she explored spirituality outside her tradition, her pastor friend's support, belief in her, and acts of justice on her behalf have enabled her to begin carving out a spiritual life that works well for her.

Nancy told of how, years after her assault, a female minister from her former denomination took a risk and went out of her way to apologize to Nancy for the way the denomination had treated her. This brought some healing to Nancy. It is never too late for religious leaders to reach out to laborers in compassion.

If you are a religious leader who knows someone who has been victimized, why not contact her by picking up the phone, sending her an email, or mailing her a letter. But before you do so, realize that your words must be followed by actions. Some of the laborers in this research spoke of kind words religious leaders had said to them, but the words were not backed by actions. Inaction is perceived by the laborer as collusive. It takes a lot of time for leaders to work with laborers, but in reality, what is more important in ministry than a commitment to being present to the broken-hearted?

The Telling and Hearing of Stories

Laborers heal when their stories are allowed to be told and are heard by others. When told in safe settings, the story not only empowers the storyteller, but changes the listener in the hearing. This was most evident in Juliana's account of signing a silencing agreement and how being limited in sharing her story prohibited her healing. It should be noted that in order for stories to have this healing property, they must be shared in safe settings with others who are open to hearing them. When laborers' stories are told in hostile environments or to a judgmental audience, retraumatization occurs.

Feminist theory and narrative approach[64] have ramifications for congregations where clergy sexual assault has occurred. Often, the assault and the removal of the clergyperson become hushed, and congregants pretend nothing has happened. Evidence of this tendency in congregations was seen in chapter 12, "A Minister's Soliloquy," when the minister states that after clergy sexual assault occurred in his congregation, he heard people say, "Move along. Least said, sooner forgotten." Congregants are often discouraged from sharing their stories or the pain they feel at being betrayed by their clergyperson.

Clergy sexual assault can be a frightening issue for congregants to work through because it prompts questions such

---

[64] For a thorough explanation of feminist theory and narrative approach please see Appendix A.

as, "If my clergyperson was not who I believed him to be, then is God who I believe God to be?" This can be a frightening question to explore, especially if the congregant now feels distrustful toward members of the clergy. Clergy sexual assault can also bring to the surface past sexual traumas for congregants, wounds which, in some cases, have been deeply buried and never addressed.

As difficult and as painful as it is to discuss clergy sexual assault in the congregation, it is necessary to do so in order for the congregation to heal and to establish healthy pastoral boundaries. Failure to do this sets the stage for the cycle of abuse to continue, as the congregation may call a clergyperson sometime in the future who turns out to be another abuser. With some regularity, congregations where assault has occurred also have histories of previous clergy committing boundary violations or acts of pastoral misconduct, such as embezzlement. The use of feminist theory and narrative approach within the congregational context enables congregants to share their stories, learn from one another's pain, create an accurate history, and take healing action by defining boundaries to create a healthier congregation.

It should be stressed that if a laborer chooses to remain within her congregation, attempts must be made to welcome her and honor her desire, or lack thereof, to tell her story. I am aware of several congregations where, in the wake of clergy sexual assault, storytelling was permitted. This was possible with the help of trained mediators who listened privately to people on all sides of the issue, compiled an overall report, and shared it publicly. Of utmost importance in each case was the fact that the laborer's story was honored. As painful as the process was, and despite the ultimate loss of some members, at least one of these congregations has since grown by leaps and bounds.

Just Action, Fewer Lawsuits

Most women do not want to sue their denomination, but when they fail to receive the support they need, they feel forced to hire a lawyer, not only to gain a sense of justice, but as an attempt to reform the church so future laborers will be treated more humanely. However, the idea of being sued seems to fuel fear among denominational and congregational leaders. This fear causes leaders on some level to objectify the woman as a threat and, as a result, to treat her unjustly and inhumanely.

Efforts must be made by congregations in the community where clergy sexual assault has occurred to support those who have been victimized and to address the ramifications of the assault in a healing manner in the congregation.[65] Although laborers do desire such support, they may not be at an emotional place where they can ask for it.

Among laborers interviewed for this research, those who had experienced restorative justice tended to retain their traditional faith and spiritual practices and feel that a deeper faith grew out of the experience. They also tended not to languish spiritually for years. Such was the case when Lindsay's former pastor was sentenced to forty years in prison and people who had belonged to the congregation where the assault occurred supported her.

Another way of treating a woman justly would be to help her find a supportive congregation and clergyperson, if she so

---

[65] For more information on the importance of addressing assault in the congregation, see the section on "Narrative Approach" in Appendix A.

desires to move to a new congregation. Many laborers find it frightening to walk into a congregation after they have been assaulted and then blamed. Attending a new church or her current one along with a denominational support person would likely make this much less traumatizing. It would be fairly easy for the denomination to assign a volunteer to support a laborer in her congregation or help her find a new church. This small act of care would validate her pain and be paramount to restoring her dignity and aiding in her rebirth. If a laborer chooses not to attend a church at this point, the volunteer could support her by offering to meet with her on a regular basis to hear and validate her story.

When a woman has a career in the church, is pursuing education toward such a career, or has plans to pursue such education, steps must be taken to ensure that she receives the needed support to continue in her career if she so chooses. In addition, the church should, at a minimum, cover the cost of counseling for women without insurance coverage. The church also must be supportive of the laborer's children and husband, though not at the expense of the laborer, who is the primary victim. (An example of "supporting" the laborer's family at her expense was the hurtful way in which a woman from Amy's congregation told her she was glad Amy was taking medication that might "knock out her sex drive," and then told Amy's husband, "I'm sorry for what happened to you.")

In addition, the wider church should make efforts to connect laborers with one another so they can support each other's healing. Good grief, do we expect people with cancer to refrain from talking and forming friendships with others who have cancer? Do we expect widows or widowers to grieve without the support of those who have grieved before them? Then why do denominations refuse to connect laborers with each other? They, too, need the support of people who have endured similar struggles.

Above all, a laborer should *never, ever* be expected to sign a silencing agreement. Asking her to do so prohibits her ability to heal, and she remains stuck. Healing occurs when we talk about our pain. Intimacy with our friends and family can only happen when we are free to discuss that which weighs heavily on our hearts. Remember what happened when Juliana broke her silencing agreement? Healing occurred and relationships were restored. Laurie's husband told me that she also signed such an agreement. In both cases, the agreement was intended to protect the offender's and the denomination's reputation, but resulted in further trauma for the laborers.

Not only does the inability to talk about clergy sexual assault impact the laborer and her relationships, but in actuality it negatively impacts the entire denomination. Silence breeds an environment for future assaults to occur. Laurie's husband explained that the silencing agreement was specifically designed so "she couldn't . . . inform the church or anybody that it happened in [Joe's] past history." As a congregant, would you want a sexual predator to serve as your clergyperson? How would you feel if the denomination knew he was a predator and not only prevented that fact from being known but allowed him to continue in his ministry at your congregation?

If you are in a position of religious leadership and it is suggested that the laborer will need to sign such an oppressive document, realize that having her do so is akin to shackling her in chains. If you are asked to support such a position, don't do it, even if the denominational attorneys want it done. Have some backbone! Stand for what is right and just, not only for the sake of the laborer, but of the entire denomination. Protecting clergy offenders serves no one's best interest.

Prevention

To keep clergy sexual assault from occurring, awareness and prevention training—for the "people in the pews" as well as leaders—needs to become a priority for denominations. Without knowledge of this crime, congregants do not have the ability to name or recognize it; nor do they know how to respond when it occurs.

To raise consciousness among the laity about this problem, volunteers could staff information booths or tables at national and local denominational conferences, as well as at youth gatherings. Information on clergy sexual assault can be included in denominational magazines, newspapers, and newsletters. Presenting information in multiple forms is necessary because abusive clergy tend to keep literature regarding clergy sexual assault out of their congregations.

Not one of the participants in this study mentioned informational literature available to their congregation or preventative training taking place at their church prior to their assault. Not one mentioned knowing what clergy sexual assault was prior to their assault. The laity needs to be educated on this crime. In addition, many of the participants stated that, had such information been available, perhaps someone would have recognized the assault for what it was, and perhaps the blaming and collusion that followed would have been less intense. Some even mentioned that, had they known about clergy sexual assault, they might have been in a position to recognize it when it began to happen to them, and to stop it early in the grooming stages (as described in chapter 13, when the pastor kissed the woman and she went after him, calling his action inappropriate).

Clergy and seminarians would benefit greatly from reading books and attending trainings on clergy sexual assault, transference, and counter-transference in counseling situations.[66] It must be acceptable for clergy to talk with an appropriate confidante (a colleague, mentor, denominational leader, etc.) about their feelings of counter-transference, such as their sexual attraction and feelings of love toward congregants. Clergy must recognize that these feelings can arise while counseling and know where to go for help with such issues without fear of being judged. At such trainings it might be helpful to have a laborer speak about her experience of how the assault impacted her life. Hearing firsthand about the damage clergy sexual assault causes just might prevent someone from inflicting such pain.

Laborers are valuable assets to congregations and denominations. Their experience of clergy sexual assault, their healing, and the wisdom they have gained by surviving the assault experience should be sought out by denominations to help in planning prevention programs, to aid when disclosure is made to other local congregations, to befriend laborers who are struggling to piece together their lives, and to speak publicly of their assaults. Many laborers interviewed for this research expressed their willingness to speak in churches about their experience in order to help prevent clergy sexual assault from

---

[66] For a further explanation of transference and counter-transference issues see Kenneth S. Pope, Janet L. Sonne, and Jean Holroyd, *Sexual Feelings in Psychotherapy: Explorations for Therapists and Therapists-in-Training* (Washington, DC: American Psychological Association, 1995); Candace R. Benyei, *Understanding Clergy Misconduct in Religious Systems* (New York: Haworth Pastoral Press, 1998).

happening to other women. In addition, the fact that laborers interpret Scripture and other sacred writings through the lens of clergy sexual assault can add diversity to congregational Bible studies and discussions.

Denominations need to work together with their sister denominations and state legislatures to ensure that clergy sexual assault will not be tolerated and will be criminally prosecuted. A global, interfaith discussion needs to occur regarding sexual violence perpetrated by members of the clergy against both women and children, and the unjust way in which virgins and laborers are treated throughout the world. We need to create awareness concerning the particularly severe struggles faced by women in patriarchal societies as they seek to overcome sexual violence. Information on clergy sexual assault and support for laborers living in patriarchal societies can be provided via the internet. Congregations and denominations can also support organizations, such as Amnesty International and Avaaz, which strive to strengthen the status of women around the world.

Faith communities joining together can make a significant difference, not just locally, but nationally and internationally.

Chapter 17

Mental Health Service Providers

All eighteen women who were interviewed for this book sought counseling due to their assault, yet not all found it helpful. To be helpful, therapists need to understand both the boundary violation and the spiritual abuse. Helpful therapists assisted laborers in realizing they were not responsible for the assault, allowed them to express anger at God, and gave laborers permission to explore alternative spiritual practices.

Currently, cognitive behavior therapies (CBT) are the evidence-based approaches that work best in treating PTSD and depression.[67] However, one laborer shared that she found CBT only minimally helpful when the counselor used it to address PTSD and suicidal tendencies because the approach ignored her underlying spiritual crisis and sense of isolation. On the other hand, not all laborers were ready to explore the existential and spiritual aspects of the assault, and at least one found CBT helpful in addressing her difficulty completing the tasks of daily living.

Some laborers found Jungian psychology helpful because it enabled them to learn how to interpret and trust the wisdom and guidance in their dreams. Those who had received Jungian therapy tended to base decisions on the guidance of

---

[67] Katrina A. Vickerman and Gayla Margolin, "Rape Treatment Outcome Research: Empirical Findings and State of the Literature," *Clinical Psychology Review* 29 (2009): 431-448.

their dreams rather than looking to an outside authority figure for such guidance.

Spiritual Crisis

Some of the laborers in this book stated that their spiritual crisis was not addressed in counseling. Others were encouraged to participate in organized religion. These methods failed to give credence to the spiritual crisis of the laborer. Social scientists Peter Madsen Gubi and Rachel Jacobs[68] found that therapists who worked with spiritually abused clients often felt the need to defend God or influence the conversation when they became uncomfortable with the spiritual direction in which the client was headed. For this reason, therapists need to be aware of when a client's spiritual crisis threatens their own beliefs so they can take action to address their own apprehensions without getting in the way of the client's healing work. Referring a laborer to a clergyperson for spiritual guidance so it does not have to be addressed in counseling is most likely not a viable option, especially if the laborer has experienced collusion after the assault.

A spiritual director may be helpful to therapists in working through their spiritual and religious apprehensions. The word "director," as used in spiritual direction, does not imply that the director takes control and *directs* the directee. Rather, the spiritual director acts as a spiritual mentor. Just as a psychotherapist attends to the inner world of her client, a

---

68 Peter Madsen Gubi and Rachel Jacobs, "Exploring the Impact on Counsellors of Working with Spiritually Abused Clients," *Mental Health, Religion and Culture* 12 (2009):191-204.

spiritual director attends to the activity of Spirit or God in the directee's life.[69]

It might also be helpful for therapists to be comfortable with religious and spiritual practices that differ from their own or, at the very least, to give laborers permission to look outside their faith traditions for spiritual nourishment. Several of the participants in this study felt that receiving permission to explore other belief systems was an important step in their rebirth. The need some laborers have for permission to explore outside their tradition most likely stems from the warnings most religions give, at least to some degree, about the dangers of seeking spiritual nourishment outside one's tradition.

Additional Findings

Five other findings from this research pertain to counseling. First, some laborers had difficulty separating the good aspects of the abusive clergyperson from the bad. For example, Amy struggled with this dilemma because she felt unable to claim any of the positive statements the abusive pastor had made concerning her in their counseling sessions. The pain of the abuse made her feel that the good things he had said were not true.

A second counseling-related area was that some of the laborers who were being counseled by the clergyperson when the assault took place still had not resolved the original issue for which they had sought counsel. The assault had preempted work on their original issue, and now that they were engaged with a new therapist, they were processing the clergy assault

---

[69] David G. Benner, "Nurturing Spiritual Growth," *Journal of Psychology and Theology* 30 (2002): 355-361.

and the original issue was left unresolved. For example, Jessica was seeking help regarding her sexual orientation when she was assaulted. At the time of our interview, she was working with a new therapist but had not yet been ready to explore her sexual orientation with that therapist. She had put her sexuality on hold, impacting her ability to move forward in an intimate relationship while she worked on processing the assault. Other laborers mentioned similar scenarios.

Third, in cases where counseling was paid for by the denomination, it tended to be short-term and not extensive enough to work through the ramifications of the assault, let alone any preexisting issue. The loss of employment resulted in some laborers losing their insurance and, therefore, being unable to pay for necessary therapy. The inability to receive therapy was one variable that affected the length of time the laborer spent rebirthing. Therefore, it might be helpful to offer group sessions for laborers. If not enough women are available to form a group specific to clergy sexual assault, laborers and adults who were sexually abused as children by members of the clergy can be combined in the same group. Laborers can also benefit from a trauma group or an incest survivors group.

An incest survivors group might be helpful because clergy sexual assault shares many similarities with incest. Candace R. Benyei writes, in her book *Understanding Clergy Misconduct,*[70] about the similarities between clergy sexual misconduct and incest. Both take place in the context of a family. In incest, the abuse is usually perpetrated by the father in the nuclear family. In clergy sexual assault, the abuse is perpetrated by the parental figure of the faith family who in

---

[70] Candace R. Benyei, *Understanding Clergy Misconduct in Religious System.* (New York: Haworth, Pastoral Press, 1998).

some religious contexts is called Father, Mother, Brother, or Sister. Society's concept of both nuclear families and church families is that they are nurturing. Yet, when a family member comes forward with an accusation of sexual abuse in an unhealthy family, that person is usually shunned from the family, just as a laborer is often shunned from her church family. Because of the similarities between incest and clergy sexual assault, laborers might be good candidates for incest survivors groups.

Fourth, others who may be in need of counseling after clergy sexual assault include the laborer's family, the congregation, the other clergy and staff in the congregation, and the abusive clergy and his family.

Finally, when laborers file a complaint with their denomination, seek mediation with religious leaders, or confront the offending clergyperson, a therapist or advocate can attend these meetings to help support, protect, and advocate on behalf of the laborer, should blaming and shaming occur. Prior to meeting with church officials, advocates should be aware that religious leaders might be manipulative, as several laborers in this study spoke of how their therapists were surprised by the degree of collusion on the part of religious leaders when they sought to get involved with the denomination on the laborer's behalf.

This was the case with Laurie sitting alone in a room with the bishop and his men and being asked about her undergarments. It was also the case when Jane went to speak with the bishop and ended up giving a deposition. Yasmine, Karen, Sharon, Dee, and I experienced similar manipulation. Because this type of violation appears to be the norm when a laborer meets with leaders from her denomination, it is best for her to play it safe and bring an advocate.

Chapter 18

Legislative Advocacy

Most laborers reported trusting congregational and denominational leaders to seek appropriate redress of the violation at the time they filed a grievance. However, nearly all of these instances resulted in collusion and retraumatization of the laborer, demonstrating that denominations are doing a poor job of policing themselves. For this reason, state-level legislation is needed throughout the United States and several of the states that have enacted legislation need to update it.

Of the eighteen women who were interviewed for this book, one brought criminal charges against the offending clergyperson, and five other laborers consulted lawyers regarding the filing of a civil suit. Of those six cases, one pastor is serving a forty-year prison sentence. Two laborers received a settlement. Two others talked with attorneys, began legal procedures, and then decided not to pursue them because the collusion intensified and pursuing legal action created more trauma and anxiety for them. One did not specify how her legal situation ended.

Criminal Sexual Assault

Currently, "only [thirteen] states and the District of Columbia have penal statutes that, in at least some circumstances, support the criminal prosecution of clergypersons engaged in sexual misconduct with congregants or parishioners."[71] However, some of these statutes are at risk of being found unconstitutional because they address the abusive counseling relationship. When the counseling relationship is deemed to have a religious or spiritual component, the courts view it as an entanglement issue with the First Amendment, which concerns the separation of church and state. Under the First Amendment, the government and its courts cannot legally dictate what happens within religious contexts.[72]

Bradley J. B. Toben and Kris Helge of Baylor University's School of Law hold the Arkansas code up as a model statute because it avoids the entanglement issue by focusing on the position of trust and authority the clergyperson holds rather than on his or her spiritual or religious role.[73] The Arkansas Code has survived legal challenge in a trial that concluded with a favorable ruling for the victim. The Arkansas Code reads:

---

[71] "These statues, enacted by Arkansas, Connecticut, Delaware, Iowa, Kansas, Minnesota, New Mexico, North Dakota, Texas, South Dakota, Utah, Wisconsin and the District of Columbia turn on various linguistic formulations, including most commonly, the specification that the misconduct occur within the confines of the counseling relationship. Only a handful of state penal statutes, to be discussed, address clergyperson sexual misconduct *outside* of the context of the counseling relationship." Bradley, J.B. Toben and Kris Helge, "Sexual Misconduct of Clergypersons with Congregants or Parishioners - Civil and Criminal Liabilities and Responsibilities." (2011): 3-4. www.baylor.edu/clergysexualmisconduct/index.php?id=63297.

[72] For an in depth analysis of this entanglement issue see Ibid, or Mark A. Weitz, *Clergy Malpractice in America: Nally v. Grace Community Church of the Valley* (Lawrence: University of Kansas, 2001).

[73] Bradley J.B. Toben and Kris Helge, "Sexual Misconduct of Clergypersons," 27.

> A person commits sexual assault in the third degree if the person engages in sexual intercourse or deviate sexual activity with another person who is not the actor's spouse, and the actor is a member of the clergy and is in a position of trust or authority over the victim and uses the position of trust or authority to engage in sexual intercourse or deviate sexual activity.[74]

Notice how the code makes no reference to clergy counseling or to the spiritual or religious nature of the clergy position.

State legislators need to be lobbied to pass laws that are constitutional, protect vulnerable adults, and give laborers the ability to file criminal charges. Because advocacy is an important part of rebirth, laborers can become involved in lobbying their state legislators to pass such legislation. In states with current laws that may be found to be unconstitutional due to emphasis on the spiritual or religious role of the clergy, laborers can advocate to amend these laws using constitutional language. Mental health professionals can also advocate political action through their national and state organizations. For example, social workers can do this through the National Association of Social Workers.

Denominational Support

Support is also needed from members of the clergy and denominational leaders to ensure that such legislation is passed in all fifty states. By way of illustration, in the state of

---

74 ARK. CODE ANN. § 5-14-126 (Supp. 2007).

Michigan in 1995, former Michigan State Representative Jon Jellema sponsored a bill to make it a fourth-degree criminal offense for mental health professionals, including clergy, to sexually exploit their clients. Although the bill passed in the House with strong support, it did not pass in the Senate because "various members of the clergy—from different faiths—came to testify against the bill. . . . [They stated] it doesn't happen, and when it does, we handle it ourselves. . . . Eventually . . . members of the committee made it clear . . . they would *not* support [the bill] if the reference to clergy remained in it."[75] When reference to members of the clergy was removed from the bill, the law readily passed.

Because of what happened in Michigan, I contend that denominational and clergy support should be established and demonstrated from the start when lobbying for such legislation in order to counter the opposition that may arise from some corners of the clergy ranks.

Justice

There is no doubt that healing is aided when justice is served. For example, Lindsay was a victim in a criminal lawsuit in which the offending pastor was convicted and sentenced to a forty-year prison sentence. She is the only woman who was interviewed who stated she did not believe she had undergone a severe spiritual crisis due to her assault. She also experienced a lesser degree of collusion from the church than did the other women interviewed. Perhaps this is because when criminal sexual assault charges were filed against the pastor, many congregants left the church, and those who left tended to

---

[75] Jon Jellema, email messages to author, March 29, 2007 and May 6, 2012.

support Lindsay and the other women who had been victimized. After all, the police had arrested the pastor, sending a pretty clear message as to who was at fault.

In cases in which disclosure was made to the congregation but no criminal charges were filed, members of the congregation tended to blame the woman and cover up or minimize the actions of the clergyperson.

Lindsay also spoke of the prosecutor's Victim Assistance Program, which paid for such things as counseling, medication, lost wages, and hospitalization for those who had been victimized. These are healing elements that the church frequently fails to provide laborers to help with their emotional and spiritual healing and to offset the financial hardship in which laborers often find themselves. While the majority of the laborers said collusion was the most damaging part of the assault, Lindsay's case illustrates how the carrying out of legal justice and restorative actions can result in a lesser degree of damage to the laborer's soul.

If legislation is passed making clergy sexual assault a criminal sexual offense in all fifty states, laborers may more readily report the assault to the police, reducing the need for denominations to conduct investigations, trials, and disciplinary procedures and, thus, also reducing denominational leaders' fear of reaching out to laborers. Such legislative changes may also decrease the likelihood of laborers being retraumatized by their communities because the clergyperson will be recognized as a convicted sex offender.

Chapter 19

Future Research

Research on healing after clergy sexual assault is scarce, and many areas remain uninvestigated. The research for this book was exploratory, meaning that there has not been much prior research on this topic. In conducting this research, I discovered many areas related to healing that call for further exploration.

Humanism, Polytheism, and Other Belief Systems

The first such area involves laborers who belong to humanistic traditions. For example, one participant who came from a more humanistic background, as opposed to the three Abrahamic religions,[76] had different healing issues than other laborers did. Whereas the three Abrahamic religions consider accountability to God key to ethical and moral behavior, humanistic traditions tend not to believe in a deity, so they see human beings as accountable to themselves and the greater good. This laborer did not struggle with the image of God or spirituality, but rather with a lack of faith in humanity and with the meaning of justice. She also mentioned that she saw a

---

[76] Judaism, Christianity, and Islam make up the Abrahamic religions because they all trace their origins back to the patriarch Abraham and the covenant made between Abraham and God.

therapist who specialized in clergy sexual abuse and "felt like this therapist lumped [her] in with everyone else who experienced [such] abuse." This difference in experience would seem to indicate the need for additional research to examine how laborers belonging to humanistic traditions differ from those who identify with Judaism, Christianity, and Islam.

Furthermore, research is needed with laborers who belong to faiths such as Buddhism, Hinduism, and the Neo-Pagan religions, like Wicca, Shamanism, and Druidism, to determine whether different healing issues present for them.

Choosing Not to Report

Not all laborers report their assault. This was true of two of the women interviewed for this book. Although they had not reported the assault, both women felt estranged from the church and struggled spiritually. It appears that some of their struggles have been similar to those of women who report and find no support within the clergy ranks. A larger sample is needed to determine if there is indeed a similarity.

High-Achievers

A number of laborers in this study went on for further education after their assault. Several held more than one master's degree, and two had done or were doing doctoral work. I became aware of this pattern of laborers returning to school while analyzing the data after completing the interviewing process, so the laborers were not directly asked about their educational background. In a number of cases, the laborer shared that she was successful academically. Two of the laborers told about their fantastic gardens, and two were talented artists.

Carol Rambo-Ronai, a social scientist and university professor, writes of a student with whom she experiences counter-transference due to their similar abusive backgrounds.[77] She tells of his "overachievement" and "perfectionism," relating these characteristics to the trauma of childhood sexual abuse he had suffered. She states that sexual abuse survivors often respond to their experiences by becoming overachievers. A study might be warranted to determine if laborers do indeed tend to become high-achievers, if clergy tend to target overachieving women, or if such women tend to participate in research to a greater extent than others.

Cultural Diversity

Although this study was somewhat diverse in terms of monotheistic denominational backgrounds represented, it was not as racially diverse as it could have been.

Mark Chaves and Diana Garland found that the prevalence of clergy sexual assault was greater among African Americans than among Caucasian Americans. Angela, the sole African American laborer in my research, stated, "In the African American church, the way [we] put [clergy] up on the pedestal is, we treat him like God." The woman interviewed in chapter 13, "A Voice from the Congregation," is also African American; she echoes Angela's sentiment. Anne M. Pope, a regional director for the New York State NAACP, confirms that

[77] Carol Rambo-Ronai, "An Unloaded Gun: Negotiating the Boundaries of Identity, Incest, and Student/Teacher Relationships," (unpublished).

this high regard of clergy is common within African American churches.[78] The fact that clergy are placed on such a pedestal may intensify the collusion African American laborers experience. Because the African American sample size in my study was unintentionally limited to one, it is impossible to state, based on this research alone, whether the severe collusion Angela experienced was an isolated incident or a common occurrence among African American laborers.

Yasmine, from the Middle East, spoke of living in a patriarchal society and the inability to find anyone who was willing to listen to her about the assault. This inability to be heard extended even to Yasmine's experiences with the mental health professionals she turned to for help. Yasmine felt isolated and ended up seeking support through internet contacts.

In addition, Ladan Alomar's insights regarding the experience of Hispanic laborers are relevant to cultural diversity among laborers. Writing in the *Journal of Religion and Abuse*, she discusses how Spanish contains many colloquial phrases relating to God, such as "Si Dios quiere [God willing]." This God-language has triggering implications for Spanish-speaking laborers in everyday communication.[79] Further research is needed with racial and cultural minorities to learn about the various healing issues that may present for them.

Children

Many of the participants who had children at the time of the assault spoke of the damage their children incurred be-

---

[78] Anne M. Pope, "A Response to Clergy Sexual Abuse: An African American Perspective," *Journal of Religion and Abuse* 5 (2004): 79-85.
[79] Ladan Alomar, "A Response to Clergy Sexual Abuse: A Latina Perspective," *Journal of Religion and Abuse* 5 (2004): 75 -77.

cause of the clergy sexual assault and the collusion which followed. Because children are at earlier stages of faith and psychosocial development, and because they might not yet have acquired a firm spiritual foundation, their spiritual healing likely takes a different course than that of an adult. Moreover, this research did not include adults who were victims of clergy sexual abuse during childhood. Research on spiritual healing needs to be done with both these populations. It might also be valuable to compare and contrast the spiritual healing of children abused by clergy and children who witnessed the effects of their mother's abuse.

The Therapy Relationship

This study did not examine the specifics of the relationship between laborers and their therapists, although some laborers shared information about it. A study that closely examines building trust in the counseling relationship after a boundary violation is warranted, as are studies regarding best-practice approaches for working with laborers.

Female Clergy

Instances have been recorded of female clergy who are sexually assaulted by a congregant. Such occurrences are not clergy sexual assault. Although I am aware of one case of a female clergyperson who was raped and then defrocked, such was a miscarriage of justice. The female clergyperson was victimized and should not be blamed for the assault. On the other hand, if she had initiated sexual contact, she would indeed be at fault. Female clergy are as responsible as male clergy for maintaining proper professional boundaries. It is outside the scope of this book to fully explore these issues, but further research is warranted.

Broad After-Effects of Clergy Sexual Assault

Little, if any, research has been conducted regarding the farther-reaching ramifications of clergy sexual assault. For instance, how does serving as an "after-pastor"—a clergyperson called or hired by a congregation where clergy sexual assault has taken place—affect him or her? Whether or not the after-pastor is informed about the prior clergy sexual assault, it can be extremely draining, emotionally and spiritually, to deal with the dynamics of such a congregation. Studies are also needed regarding the impact of assault on members of the congregation.

Care and Treatment of Abusive Clergy

Finally, further research is warranted on preventative measures with and treatment outcomes of clergy who have demonstrated abusive tendencies. Often, denominations either transfer them to other ministry settings or cast them out altogether. Neither approach is beneficial or truly addresses the behavior.

Furthermore, research is needed to determine best practices for caring for and counseling the offender's family, who have also suffered greatly.

Afterword:

Together, Let's Fight the Good Fight

Fight the good fight . . .
to which you were called. . . .

—1 Timothy 6:12 (NRSV)

Even as I finish preparing *Fighting the Good Fight* for publication, I continue to be contacted by women who desire to be interviewed for my research. After telling them the research has been completed, I have accepted the opportunity to listen to some of their stories of assault and collusion. Two of these women were assaulted by pastors in my former denomination. As a result of the assault, one is battling to retain her clergy credentials while the offender was able to transfer to another position. The second was retraumatized by denominational officials, including onc working directly with misconduct prevention. Sometimes I become frustrated with the denomination because change is so slow in coming; in the meantime, people continue to be hurt and lives are needlessly disrupted.

It is easy to become caught up in frustration and anger. However, upon further investigation, I have learned there is more to the story. There always is.

About the same time I spoke with the two women mentioned above, I attended the "Healthy Boundaries for Clergy and Spiritual Teachers" facilitator training taught by Dr. Marie

Fortune and others from the FaithTrust Institute. Four faculty from the Lutheran School of Theology at Chicago (LSTC), the seminary from which I graduated, were also in attendance, preparing to provide seminary students with the latest information in boundary training. My editor, Heidi Mann, who worked diligently on this book and was supportive of me along my healing journey, was a seminary classmate of mine, is an ordained clergyperson, and wants change just as much as I do.

Although collusion is found in all denominations, also found are people committed to justice and who are working diligently to bring about needed reforms. Each person interviewed for this book has played a part in working toward such reform.

Janet's rabbi-mentor gave her the charge that she had been drafted to the battlefield. If you have read this far in *Fighting the Good Fight*, you have also been drafted. What will you do to make a difference in this battle? If you feel unsure of where to begin, follow a suggestion from section IV or elsewhere in the book that resonates most with you, and go from there. Even if it seems like a small step—saying a friendly "hello" to a laborer or sharing this book with a pastor or bishop or church member you know—it will surely make a difference. In time, you may feel led to do more.

If you are a sister-laborer (or a brother-laborer), struggling and feeling isolated, please know you are not alone. Healing from clergy sexual assault is possible. I hope you can view the women profiled in this book—and me—as a demonstration of that. It hasn't been easy for any of us, and it won't be for you either. But it will get better. Although you may have turned to many for help and been revictimized, numerous people *are* available to support you.

Early in my rebirth, I attended a retreat for survivors of clergy sexual abuse. One of our group activities was to get a horse to walk through a maze we had created. We needed to work together, could not speak to one another, and could not touch the horse. If the horse made a mistake and stepped outside the maze, we had to return to the beginning and start over. We spent several hours diligently trying to achieve the goal but never managed to do so.

Eventually, the facilitator told us it was time to stop. She then said she had never seen a group so committed to finishing the task. Her previous groups had always given up. She thought our sheer determination bore testimony to how persistently we had each faced seemingly insurmountable obstacles in seeking justice in our religious institutions.

I share this story because talking about clergy sexual abuse and assault with people in the church often feels like talking to the back end of a horse, with little if anything ever changing. Yet laborers continue seeking justice from the institutions that traumatized them, and there *are* people within the institutions who want to see and are working toward reform.

If you are "fighting the good fight," interested in getting involved in the fight, or looking for further support or information, please visit carolynwaterstradt.com, where you will find links to helpful resources and will be able to stay current on this very important issue. It is my desire that if you have suffered clergy sexual assault, you will find healing through the love and support of others along your journey to rebirth.

Healing is possible. You are not alone.

We can make a difference and change the world. Together, let's fight the good fight.

Warmly,
Carolyn

SECTION V:

Appendices, Gratitude, and Resources

Appreciation is a wonderful thing:
It makes what is excellent in others belong to us as well.

—Voltaire

Appendix A:

Theories Behind the Research

A postmodern, social constructivist perspective was used in writing this book. A core concept of postmodernism is that people know the world indirectly through their perceptions, while constructivists further view these perceptions as stemming from what culture and society consider normal. This idea of normal is, in turn, adopted by the individuals living within any given culture or social group. In choosing to use a constructivist approach, I aim to shift the focus from the blame that the offending clergy and many religious organizations place on laborers to the stories the women themselves tell of their strengths.

Feminist Theory

I let feminist theory guide the interview process because it values each woman's story, emphasizes women's experiences, and claims the strength found in each woman.[80] This research focused on the lived experiences of laborers, who told stories of marginalization and of their attempts to survive and even triumph over systemic oppression. For many, part of their healing was finding empowerment in advocacy work and in learning new skills, such as gardening or artwork. The study

---

[80] Shantih E. Clemans, "A Feminist Group for Women Rape Survivors," *Social Work with Groups* 28 (2005): 59-75.

participants also expressed hope, and it was an underlying desire of mine, that these stories would be made available to other women who are struggling with the aftermath of clergy sexual assault, offering them messages of hope and camaraderie.

Feminist theory stresses the importance of allowing the disenfranchised to speak for themselves without interpretation by the researcher. In order to do this, feminists often present their findings using poetry, plays, artwork, dance, and music. The art gives expression to the soul of the storyteller, and it is the soul which yearns for expression in laborers' lives.

Yasmine, from the Middle East, experienced blatant forms of sexism. In the United States, the sexism experienced by laborers was more subtle. Yet traces of it were evident in every woman's story. Because sexism is ingrained in religious traditions, it often goes unnoticed. It is important that both misogynistic concepts of clergy sexual assault and sacred stories be reinterpreted through a feminist and narrative lens. Although this is being done by feminist theologians, these theologies, to a great extent, remain ignored or unknown in most congregations. It is well past time for these theologies to be taught to the laity.

Narrative Approach

In using narrative approach, the problem is placed outside the storyteller. This means that the problem is not the storyteller, but rather the untrue stories told about her. In the case of laborers, the problem is the assault, along with the blame and collusion which typically follow. By using narrative approach to analyze the interviews, blame-filled stories were rejected as untruths, allowing new truths and realities to emerge and be celebrated. These newly discovered truths were that the laborers were resourceful, witty, compassionate, talented, and strong. Such new labels did not fit into the dominant story many religious people tell about laborers. Therefore, new language was needed to give form to the narrative; hence, my use of the terms "virgin," "laborer," and "midwife." Additionally, John of the Cross's dark night of the soul provided a framework of spiritual development in which the laborer could place herself. Using these concepts, the laborer now becomes grounded in a new reality.

Existential Approach

Laborers often find themselves in the sort of spiritual, existential vacuum which can only be filled by attaching new meaning and purpose to one's life. In using an existential approach, I made a conscious effort to look for where the laborer had attached such new meaning. Existential approach concerns itself with the human condition and looks specifically at the meaning of life, existential anxiety, freedom and responsibility, and the certainty of death. For laborers, healing advances were made through finding new meaning and a new purpose to life.

Conclusion

In using these models for this research, it has been my intent to offer hope that all laborers have the potential for healing, through their courage to share painful memories, their determination to overcome difficult struggles, their desire to care for a broken world, and their resourcefulness to attach new meanings to spirituality and other aspects of their lives.

Appendix B:

Methods and Limitations

A qualitative research approach was taken to discover how healing takes place in adult female laborers. Specifically, an exploratory, cross-sectional survey design was used to collect data from participants. This design was chosen because there had not yet been any studies conducted regarding spiritual healing after clergy sexual assault and this design works well when no prior research has been done.

Sample Population

Snowball and convenience samples were used. News of this research project was disseminated through newsletters, emails, and websites linked with various clergy sexual abuse networks. Participants were required to be women who had been sexually abused by a clergyperson after the age of eighteen and who were not currently involved in litigation regarding their assault. Also, the abusive clergyperson had to hold a master's degree or its equivalent, which typically would mean the clergyperson had graduated from seminary; in many denominations, a master's degree is a prerequisite for ordination.

Data Collection

Because laborers are a hidden subpopulation not located in a small geographic area, data was collected primarily through individual, unstructured phone interviews which were recorded and later transcribed. Due to the illness and loss of voice of one of the participants and our inability to reschedule because of the deadline to complete the interviewing, one interview was conducted over the internet, first via a chatroom, and secondly, because of the slow process of exchanging chat messages, through email. Conducting the interview in this way allowed the interviewee to participate, and indeed, the information she provided proved significant in the overall analysis.[81]

Another interview was conducted via Skype with a participant who lives in the Middle East. Using Skype enabled us to conduct the interview at no cost, avoiding the high charges of an international phone call. This participant's voice also was important to the overall findings of this research.

Social scientist Harvey L. Gochros recommends that an unstructured interview be used when there is a lack of research in a particular area and when the area being studied is a sensitive one. Although unstructured interviewing was indeed the predominant form employed, the funneling technique, including some structured questions to collect demographic information, was used at the beginning of each interview. The funneling technique was utilized because it has "been found to be useful in gaining honest and complete

---

[81] Nalita James and Hugh Busher, "Credibility, Authenticity and Voice: Dilemmas in Online Interviewing," *Qualitative Research* 6 (2006): 403-420.

answers from research participants. . . . The advantage of this approach is that rapport can be established early in the interview with questions that do not make the interviewee particularly uncomfortable."[82]

I took into consideration ethical concerns set forth by Estelle Disch regarding doing research with people who have been sexually abused by professionals.[83] Grand Valley State University's Human Research Review Committee reviewed the protocol for this research and ensured that the methodology was ethical and protected the participants from potential harm.

About half of the participants knew I was a laborer, either because we were personal acquaintances or because they had found information on me via an internet search concerning clergy sexual assault. A few participants asked during the interview if I was a laborer, in which case I disclosed that I was and provided brief feedback to their inquires about my healing experience and the loss of my theological career. For several participants, knowledge that I had experienced clergy sexual assault and collusion helped establish rapport and trust between us, and the interview proceeded with more depth and honesty than I believe would have been possible had the participant believed I did not truly understand the shame associated with clergy sexual assault.

The interviews lasted from thirty-five minutes to three hours, with the average being seventy-five minutes. The inter-

---

[82] Harvey L. Gochros, "Qualitative Interviewing," in *Social Work Research and Evaluation: Foundations of Evidence-Based Practice*, ed. Richard M. Grinnell, Jr., and Yvonne A. Unrau (Oxford: Oxford University Press, 2008), 249.

[83] Estelle Disch, "Research as Clinical Practice: Creating a Positive Research Experience for Survivors of Sexual Abuse by Professionals," *Sociological Practice: A Journal of Clinical and Applied Sociology* 3 (2001): 221-239.

views were transcribed within a week of their occurrence, and the recordings were subsequently deleted. Identifying information, such as names, locations, and congregations, was replaced with pseudonyms. However, the ages of the laborers and denominational affiliations were not changed.

Besides the demographic questions, only one question was common to every interview: "Could you describe your spiritual life after the abuse ended?" In addition to how each participant's spirituality had been affected by the assault, I probed for how their spiritual practices and sacred images had been impacted, as well as what had been helpful and harmful in the healing process.

Data Analysis

After transcribing the interviews, I coded them line by line using open coding methods. After coding the first interview, I grouped the open codes by similarities until seven categories emerged. These categories then became the axial codes and were assigned names:

- Background Information;
- Aftermath: Harmful/Not Helpful;
- Aftermath: Helpful/Healing;
- Roles Affected by the Assault;
- Symptoms of the Assault;
- Rebirth.

Through these axial codes, I was able to chart the course of how this first participant's spirituality had changed following clergy sexual assault. Using the axial codes, I went through the coding process with the remaining seventeen interviews. New open codes were added; however no new axial codes emerged.

Once tabulated, the data was scrutinized using feminist theory and narrative and existential approaches. Through feminist theory, I searched the stories for the strength of each participant. I also searched the stories for instances of systemic, patriarchal oppression which challenged and hindered growth and healing. Through a narrative approach, I examined a new way to tell the participants' stories in a manner free of the oppressive constructs their religious community often developed about them. I also searched their stories for times when they were strong in the light of these negative, systemic narratives, enabling stories with new meaning to be constructed. As an existentialist, I looked for meaning in suffering and in the laborers' lives, as well as for the freedom of choice each has employed to free herself from the abusive relationship and move toward wholeness.

Along the way, I discovered similarities with how Viktor Frankl, in *Man's Search for Meaning*, recounts his three-year experience as a prisoner in the concentration camps during World War II, and his search for meaning in the midst of that suffering.[84] With Frankl's story in mind, I searched the laborers' stories for hints of what life expected from them.

Limitations

Four limitations should be considered. First, because all the participants were volunteers, their stories may differ from

---

[84] Viktor E. Frankl, *Man's Search for Meaning*, Boston: Beacon Press, 2006.

those who learned about the opportunity to be part of the study but chose not to participate. Second, all the data was self-reported by the participants with varying lengths of time having elapsed since the clergy sexual assault. Self-reported data is limited because the recall of the participant cannot be verified. Third, as the researcher, I interpreted the data through my own experience of clergy sexual assault, my theoretical orientations, and my theological training. Although I tried to eliminate my bias, one's bias can never be completely removed. Fourth, the findings of this study should be interpreted with care, as this was an exploratory study and a small, largely homogenous sample was used. It is not known if a larger, more diverse sample would provide the same findings.

Acknowledgements

Writing this book would not have been possible without the help, support, and encouragement of many people. First and foremost, it was an honor and a privilege to work with the women and men who had experienced clergy sexual assault and abuse and who engaged in this research endeavor. The participants' willingness to share, as well as the way in which many survivors who were unable to participate trusted me with their stories, was deeply moving. I am thankful for the participants' suggestions and edits to early versions of this manuscript and for their referrals to other sources they believed would make the book stronger. Their courage and belief in this project propelled me forward to its completion.

If not for Dr. Cray Mulder, this project would not have been undertaken. She created the safe, structured, and nurturing environment I needed in order to tackle this topic, and her passion for qualitative inquiry was contagious. Her dedication to and enthusiasm for research were the impetus for me to pursue this project. Dr. Dianne Green-Smith grounded me in theory and, through her high academic standards, challenged me always to regard the subject matter through a biopsychosocial and systems perspective. Rev. John DeBoer's theological queries encouraged me to look to my own theological roots, which, in turn, gave the book greater depth and breadth. I express my sincere appreciation to the School of Social Work faculty at Grand Valley State University in Grand Rapids, Michigan. Their support and encouragement in class projects was vital to this book. Thank you to Dr. Patty Stow Bolea, Dr. Douglas Chung, Dr. James Edwards, Dr. Jerry Johnson, Dr. Salvador

Lopez-Arias, the late Dr. Rodney Mulder, Professor Judy Gabrielse and Professor Jamie Langlois. Dr. Diana Garland and the rest of the Baylor team, your research and work around clergy sexual misconduct inspired me. Thank you also to my classmates, who encouraged me along the way.

Natalie Callesen and Susanna Mason-Defever read through the finished manuscript, offering suggestions for improvement and correcting grammatical errors. They helped make this book more concise and well-rounded. My copyeditor Rev. Heidi Mann's careful review of the manuscript produced a polished product. Amy Shamroe's help navigating the world of publishing was invaluable and made the process less scary. Tricia L. McDonald, my publisher and a valued Toastmaster colleague, offered guidance and encouragement to me throughout the publishing process. Michelle Doetsch, my accountability partner, held me accountable each day to meeting my writing and editing goals. Thank you, Brent Link, my Toastmaster colleague, for reading my thesis and for your encouragement as I conducted interviews. Publicizing what I was doing was scary, but your interest in the project calmed my jitters and self-doubt. The members of Community Toastmasters #3009 heard and applauded my story the first and subsequent times I publicly told it. Your feedback and support over the years instilled in me the courage to tell my story publicly and molded me with the ability to tell it effectively. Thank you, valued Toastmasters, for inspiring me throughout the years to stretch and grow in ways I never envisioned possible.

Thank you to Dot Ledrick, my spiritual director, and to Inie Bijkert, my therapist. Your guidance, direction, and acceptance equipped me with the tools I needed for survival. My appreciation goes to Luke Seward, Bruce Spoelman, and Jeannette Bytwerk, who believed in my ability to manage a department at a time when I was unable to believe in myself. Luke and Jeannette, thank you for listening to me on the days at work when I struggled with the assault, and thank you for your belief in this book. Thank you also to the entire Muskegon Family YMCA staff who became a supportive and healing community for my children, who had experienced much community rejection. Your dedication to the YMCA's mission and core values definitely builds healthy spirits, minds, and bodies.

Thank you to Rev. Vince Lavieri, who filled in the rest of the story, offered his friendship, and became my brother on the road to rebirth. Veronica Fierros, you are a true sister always and forever. Marcia Weeden, your belief in the book and your support and encouragement over the years made completion of this project possible. Kryssis Diane Bjork, thank you for your friendship and inclusion of me in the interfaith community. I also express appreciation to Bishop Gary Hanson and Rev. Rebecca Ebb-Speese, who were always ready to listen, and did everything in their power to bring justice to my situation. Thank you, too, to Rev. Dr. Richard Perry and Rev. Dr. Kadi Billman of the Lutheran School of Theology at Chicago, who offered their presence and encouragement when I was struggling to understand my experience while finishing seminary. Margret Bazany, shamanic practitioner extraordinaire, who retrieved small splinters of innocence which sparked new life. Rev. Lydia Warring-Meyers, I am grateful for our friendship, our many discussions on clergy sexual assault, and your support for me to get my book done! Thank you to all my friends who offered their support as I worked throughout the years on this project.

My deepest gratitude is to my family. My husband David was my biggest champion and encouraged me constantly by listening to my theories, helping me with legal jargon, and taking on full-time parenting duties at various stages of this book. My children, Abigail, Mathias, and Rebecca, graciously accepted my domination of the computer and often presented me with a much-needed reprieve; my in-laws, the Waterstradt-Olson clan, whose acceptance was paramount; my brother and sister-in-law, Nick and Thea Callesen, surrounded me with love when I was at my worst; and my parents, Natalie and Richard Callesen, taught me by their example that, regardless of the tragic losses one faces in life, life is a gift to celebrate.

Glossary

The definitions contained in this glossary explain how the following terms are used in the context of this book. For example, collusion surely takes place in various settings under various circumstances but is defined here only in relation to clergy sexual assault.

Axial codes – categories into which **open codes** are grouped in order to show relationship. For example, one of the axial codes for this research was "Aftermath: Harmful/Not Helpful." Under this code, open codes such as "blame victim," "denial," "silenced," "victim exposed," and others were placed.

Clergy – a religious or spiritual leader who has been granted authority by the overarching denomination/religious body to teach and/or preach.

Clergy sexual assault – any time a religious or spiritual leader has a sexual relationship with a congregant. Even if the congregant believes it is a consensual relationship, it is not. Because of the power differential in the relationship due to the clergyperson's religious role, a congregant can never truly give consent for a sexual relationship with a clergyperson.

Constructivism – the belief that people know the world through their perceptions of it, which in turn stem from what their culture and society deem normal.

Collusion – the inability or unwillingness of religious leaders to respond in a just fashion to clergy sexual assault. Although leaders sometimes respond to clergy sexual assault by **defrocking**, they often fail to respond to the needs of the **laborer**. Collusion can include, but is not limited to, failure to remove the clergyperson, failure to explain to the congregation that the clergyperson sexually violated the laborer, failure to find a safe place for the laborer to worship, and viewing the woman as defective because she was assaulted.

Counter-transference – the **transference** a helping professional, such as a clergyperson, sometimes projects onto a client, counselee, congregant, or other individual being served through the professional relationship. When the helping professional does not recognize his or her counter-transference issue, he or she often acts out on it unethically, such as by violating the boundaries of the relationship.

Criminal sexual assault – situations of unwanted touching, groping, attempted rape, and rape, though sexual assault penal codes vary in the U.S. according to state. Sexual assault, such as unwanted touching and groping, can occur when the victim is clothed. Criminal sexual assault also includes any sexual act in which manipulation and coercion were used.

Cross-section – a small sample that represents the whole. For example, in this research, the eighteen women interviewed were a **cross-section** of the entire population of laborers that exists at any given time.

Dark night of the soul – a period of time in which spiritual practices lose meaning for a devotee and it feels as if God has withdrawn from one's life.

Data – information collected in the course of research. The data in this research were the interviews, which were recorded, typed into transcripts, and analyzed.

Defrock – to remove a clergyperson's clergy credentials.

Denomination – segments, branches, or sects within a religion, sharing similar beliefs and practices and, often, a governing structure. For example, the Presbyterian Church (USA) is a denomination of Christianity.

Dissociation – a neurotic defense mechanism in which one detaches from outside stimuli. Dissociation occurs on a continuum from mild, common responses such as day-dreaming while driving or getting lost in a good book, to more severe responses like feeling outside one's body, not being able to access certain feelings such as anger, or feeling spaced-out. Symptoms of chronic dissociation are found in PSTD.

Entanglement issue – refers to a U.S. Supreme Court ruling that the government cannot become excessively entangled with religion. This ruling is based on the First Amendment to the U.S. Constitution and is sometimes referred to as the Lemon test because it was decided in *Lemon v. Kurtzman.*

Existentialism – a form of philosophy and psychology which centers on the human condition. Existentialism is concerned with the meaning of life, the certainty of death, existential anxiety, and freedom and responsibility.

Exploratory research – research that is done when no or very little prior research has been conducted on a subject. The research is exploratory in nature because nothing concrete is truly known about the subject.

First Amendment – the first part of the First Amendment to the U.S. Constitution concerns the separation of church and state. The entire First Amendment reads: “Congress shall make no law respecting an establishment of religion, or prohibiting the free exercise thereof; or abridging the freedom of speech, or the press; or the right of the people peaceably to assemble; and to petition the government for a redress of grievances.” U.S. courts often rule in favor of clergy or churches because laws that interfere with one’s religious rights are not allowed.

Feminist theory – a form of interpretation that examines gender inequality, oppression, women's lived experiences, and promotes women's rights and interests.

Flashback – a memory in which an event is unexpectedly revisited as vividly as if it were occurring in the present.

Funneling technique – an interviewing technique in which the easiest or least threatening questions are asked first. In this research, demographic questions were asked first, followed by a broad, open-ended question regarding spirituality after clergy sexual assault.

G-d – the manner in which many observant Jews write "God," as a way to show their respect and reverence by not fully naming the Divine Name and preventing the Divine Name from being misused. In keeping with this Jewish tradition, when the Jewish laborer speaks in this book, I use this spelling.

Grooming – the process of manipulation an offending clergyperson uses to gradually break down a woman's boundaries prior to sexual assault.

Humanism – the philosophy that views human beings as responsible for their own ethical behavior and rejects belief in a deity.

Joe – the pseudonym given in this book to all abusive clergy.

Jungian approach – psychotherapy based on the work of Carl G. Jung, often centered on dream interpretation.

Labor – the process a woman undergoes after her abusive relationship with a religious or spiritual leader ends.

Laborer – a woman who was, but is no longer, in an abusive relationship with a religious or spiritual leader.

Mandala – an art form found in Buddhism and Hinduism and popularized in the West by Carl Jung, who made mandalas a tool of psychotherapy. A mandala is a large circle that represents the self. When the circle is filled, the images contained within portray information about the artist that is not fully conscious. Mandala sketching helps bring knowledge and feelings to the surface before one is able to articulate them verbally.

Midwife – a role sometimes adopted by a laborer who has experienced some form of rebirth. Midwives labor with those in pain by allowing the wisdom of their experience to engage and support others who are hurting.

Narrative approach – a type of therapy concerned with recreating the unhealthy stories people tell about themselves. Our stories become our identity. Narrative approach hears the story and then begins to deconstruct it. As new meaning is attached to the story, it is reconstructed, making room for a new identity to emerge.

Open codes – categories into which patterns discovered in data are grouped. For example, in the research in this book, some of the open codes were "employment," "children," "blame victim," "denial," "silenced," "victim exposed," "whistle blower," "image of God," "acceptance," and "new talents." These open codes were then grouped into **axial codes**.

PTSD – post-traumatic stress disorder; an anxiety disorder which occurs in some people after they have been exposed to a traumatic event.

Patriarchy – a system in which males hold the majority of the power. Religion is often patriarchal, in that women frequently have not been allowed to be religious leaders. Even in traditions that now ordain women and elect them to ecclesiastical leadership roles, women's concerns, especially in regard to sexual discrimination, are often dismissed or not fully recognized.

Postmodern – a system of thought in which the core concepts are that truth is subjective, reality is a social construct, people know the world indirectly through their perceptions, and these perceptions are subject to change giving rise to new truths.

Qualitative research – in-depth research that explores the why and how of an issue, as opposed to quantitative research, which concerns itself with statistics and hypothesis. The research behind this book is qualitative in nature.

Rebirth – the emergence of a new self after the labor that follows clergy sexual assault.

Restorative justice – a form of justice involving all stakeholders with the goal of repairing the harm done and restoring individuals to appropriate communities of care and support. The victim's needs are considered, the offender offers to make restitution, and the community members play an active part in seeking the steps needed to transform the situation. Although an offender will not always agree to take part in such a process, it should be offered as a step in the healing process between a laborer and her congregation and denomination.

Sample – the people interviewed for a research study.

SNAP – Survivors Network for those Abused by Priests; an advocacy organization supporting survivors of clergy sexual abuse.

Soul – the essence of a person that is intimately connected with life, the Life Giver, and creation.

Soul wound – a wound that occurs when trauma shakes the core of one's being and calls into question all previously held beliefs and worldviews, making the world seem unsafe.

Spiritual direction – the ancient practice in which a trained director helps the directee discern her spiritual path and tell her spiritual story. St. John of the Cross was St. Teresa of Avila's spiritual director.

Stockholm Syndrome – a phenomenon first recognized in 1973, in which people held captive, physically or psychologically, come to identify with and empathize with their captor or abuser.

Suicidal ideation – having thoughts about suicide.

Transference – the projecting of feelings (often unconsciously) that usually stem from childhood onto a helping professional, such as a religious leader. Transference gives a false sense of connection to a person and commonly occurs in counseling relationships. Working through transference is an important aspect of counseling.

Transcribe – to type out the verbal exchange that makes up an interview.

Transcript – a typed-out record of an interview.

Trigger – an event or sensory experience which pulls one back emotionally and mentally to a traumatic time in one's life, often resulting in a physical response such as tremors, difficulty breathing, etc.

Ungrounded, to become – to lose one's emotional footing and become lost in the trauma of one's life. This may happen to a laborer frequently, interfering with her ability to perform daily activities, or it may be a momentary experience in which a laborer is unable to function for a short time as she is carried away by emotions, flash backs, or other interferences.

Unstructured interview – an interview without any pre-set format or questions.

Virgin – a woman who is in the process of being groomed for assault or is being sexually abused by a religious or spiritual leader.

Works Cited

Alomar, Ladan. "A Response to Clergy Sexual Abuse: A Latina Perspective." *Journal of Religion and Abuse,* 5 (2004): 75-77.

Arkansas Code Annotated. § 5-14-101, Supplement 2007.

Autumn, Emilie. *Opheliac.* The End Records. 2009. Compact disc.

Barks, Coleman, trans. *Rumi: The Book of Love.* San Francisco: HarperCollins, 2003.

Barrick, Audrey. "Survey Reveals Prevalence of Clergy Sexual Misconduct." *The Catholic Sentinel.* May 18, 2011.

"Beecher-Tilton Scandal." *Brown University Library.* n.d. Accessed on March 11, 2010, http://library.brown.edu/exhibits/archive/RLCexhibit/beecher/beecherms.html.

Benkert, Marianne and Thomas P. Doyle. "Clericalism, Religious Duress and Its Psychological Impact on Victims of Clergy Sexual Assault." *Pastoral Psychology* 58 (2009): 223-238.

Benner, David G. "Nurturing Spiritual Growth." *Journal of Psychology and Theology* 30 (2002): 355-361.

Benyei, Candace R. *Understanding Clergy Misconduct in Religious Systems.* New York: Haworth Pastoral Press, 1998.

Birchard, Thaddeus. "Clergy Sexual Misconduct: Frequency and Causation." *Sexual and Relationship Therapy* 15 (2000):127-139.

Brock, Rita Nakashima. *Journey by Heart: A Christology of Erotic Power.* New York: Crossroad, 1988.

Chaves, Mark and Diana R. Garland. "The Prevalence of Clergy Sexual Advance Toward Adults in Their Congregations." *Journal for the Scientific Study of Religion* 48 (2009): 817-824.

Christianson, Stephen. "Tilton v. Beecher: 1875." *Great American Trials* (2002). Accessed June 19, 2011, http://www.encyclopedia.com/doc/1G2-3498200091.htm.

Clemans, Shantih E. "A Feminist Group for Women Rape Survivors." *Social Work with Groups* 28 (2005): 59-75.

"Causes and Context Report Released on Clergy Sexual Abuse of Minors," *Catholic Sentinel,* May 18, 2011

Dart, John. "Denies Take Over Attempt: Issued Warning about Bakker, Swaggart Says." *Los Angeles Times* October 15, 1991.

Davidson, Jonathan R.T, Kathryn M. Connor, and Li-Ching Lee. "Beliefs in Karma and Reincarnation among Survivors of Violent Trauma: A Community Survey." *Social Psychiatry and Psychiatric Epidemiology* 40 (2005): 120-125.

Disch, Estelle. "Research as Clinical Practice: Creating a Positive Research Experience for Survivors of Sexual Abuse by Professionals." *Sociological Practice: A Journal of Clinical and Applied Sociology* 3 (2001): 221-239.

Evangelical Lutheran Church in America. *An ELCA Strategy for Responding to Sexual Abuse in the Church.* Chicago: Evangelical Lutheran Church in

America, 2005. http://www.elca.org/Growing-In-Faith/Vocation/Rostered Leadership/Leadership-Support/Safe-Place/General-Resources.aspx.

"FaithTrust Institute Hopes Religious Institutions Will Be Sanctuaries of Safety." *The Fig Tree.* November 2008. http://www.thefigtree.org/nov08/110108faithtrust.html

Falsetti, Sherry A. Patricia A. Resick, and Joanne L. Davis. "Changes in Religious Beliefs Following Trauma." *Journal of Traumatic Stress* 16 (2003): 391-398

Filteau, Jerry. "Report Says Clergy Sexual Abuse Brought 'Smoke of Satan' into Church." *Catholic News Service,* February 27, 2004.

Francis, Perry C. and James Stacks. "The Association between Spiritual Well-Being and Clergy Sexual Misconduct." *Journal of Religion and Abuse* 5 (2003): 79-100.

Frankl, Viktor E. *Man's Search for Meaning.* Boston: Beacon Press, 2006.

Fortune, Marie M. *Is Nothing Sacred?* Cleveland: United Church Press, 1999.

Fowler, J.W. *Stages of Faith: The Psychology of Human Development and the Quest for Meaning.* San Francisco: Harper, 1981.

Garland, Diana R. "When Wolves Wear Shepherds' Clothing: Helping Women Survive Clergy Sexual Abuse." *Social Work and Christianity* 33 (2006): 1-35.

Garland, Diana R. and Christen Argueta. "How Clergy Sexual Misconduct Happens: A Qualitative Study of First-Hand Accounts." *Social Work and Christianity* 37 (2009): 1-27.

Gernz, Stanley J. and Roy D. Bell. *Betrayal of Trust.* Grand Rapids: Baker Books, 1995.

Gochros, Harvey L. "Qualitative Interviewing." In *Social Work Research and Evaluation.* Edited by Richard M. Grinnell and Yvonne A. Unrau, 239-264. Oxford: Oxford University Press, 2008.

Gonzales, Justo. *The Story of Christianity, Volume 1.* San Francisco: Harper, 1984.

Gorski, Terence T., "PTSD in Children and Adolescents," February 1, 2002. http://www.tgorski.com/terrorism/PTSD%20In%20Children%20&%20Adolescents.htm# Posttraumatic Stress Disorder In Childhood and Adolescence: A Review.

Gubi, Peter M. and Rachel Jacobs. "Exploring the Impact on Counsellors of Working with Spiritually Abused Clients." *Mental Health, Religion and Culture* 12 (2009): 191-204.

Hall, John. "BGCT Post Clergy Registered Sex Offenders." *Baptist General Convention of Texas,* June 6, 2007.

Hawthorne, Nathaniel. *The Scarlet Letter.* New York: Bantam Dell, 2003.

James, Nalita and Hugh Busher. "Credibility, authenticity and voice: dilemmas in online interviewing." *Qualitative Research* 6 (2006): 403-420.

John of the Cross, St. *Dark Night of the Soul.* Translated by E. Allison Peers. New York: Image Books,1990.

Keene, Frederick W. "Structures of Forgiveness in the New Testament." In *Violence Against Women and Children: A Christian Theological Sourcebook*, edited by Carol J. Adams and Marie M. Fortune,121-134. New York: Continuum, 1995.

Keys, Laurinda, "Church Is No Longer Malpractice Sanctuary." *The Free Lance Star,* June 7, 1980. http://news.google.com/newspapers?nid=1298&dat=19800607&id=XOsQAAAAIBAJ&sjid=6osDAAAAIBA J&pg=5649,966928.

"Largest 25 Denominations/Communions from the 2011 Yearbook of American and Canadian Churches." *Hartford Institute for Religious Research.* http://hirr.hartsem.edu/research/fastfacts/fast_facts.html.

Leap of Faith. Directed by Richard Pearce. 1992. Hollywood, CA: Paramount Pictures, 2003. DVD.

"Major Religious Traditions in the U.S.," *The Pew Forum on Religion and Public Life.* Accessed September 25, 2011, http://religions.pewforum.org/reports.

McCullough, Colleen. *The Thorn Birds*. New York: Avon Books, 1977.

Medwick, Cathleen. *Teresa of Avila: The Progress of a Soul.* New York: Doubleday, 1999.

Minnesota Statute 1986 c 372 s 1.

Moore, Thomas. *Dark Nights of the Soul: A Guide to Finding Your Way through Life's Ordeals.* New York: Gotham Books, 2004.

Morey, Ann-Janine. "Blaming Women for the Sexually Abusive Male Pastor." *The Christian Century* 105 (1988): 866-869.

Pope, Anne M. "A Response to Clergy Sexual Abuse: An African American Perspective." *Journal of Religion and Abuse* 5 (2004): 79-85.

Pope, Kenneth S., Janet L. Sonne, and Jean Holroyd. *Sexual Feelings in Psychotherapy: Explorations for*

Therapists and Therapists-in-Training. Washington, DC: American Psychological Association, 1995.

Prendergast, Monica. "Introduction: The Phenomena of Poetry in Research." In *Poetic Inquiry: Vibrant Voices in the Social Sciences*. Edited by Monica Prendergast, Carl Leggo, Pauline Sameshima, xix-xlii. Rotterdam: The Netherlands: Sense Publishers, 2009.

Rambo-Ronai, Carol. "An Unloaded Gun: Negotiating the Boundaries of Identity, Incest, and Student/Teacher Relationships." (Unpublished.)

Rutter, Peter. *Sex in the Forbidden Zone: When Men in Power—Therapists, Doctors, Clergy, Teachers, and Others—Betray Women's Trust.* Los Angeles: Jeremy P. Tarcher, 1989.

Smith, Andrea, "Soul Wound: The Legacy of Native American Schools." *Amnesty International Magazine,* March 26, 2007.

Stevens, Darryl W, ed. *Handling Sexual Misconduct Complaints: A Handbook for United Methodist Bishops and Cabinets.* Chicago: The General Commission on the Status and Role of Women, 2011. Accessed April 29, 2011, http://www.umsexualethics.org/LinkClick.aspx?fileticket=yDFdp1qsZLw%3D&tabid=8591.

"TRIALS: The Chaplain's Case." *Time,* Monday, April 3, 1972. http://www.time.com/time/magazine/article/0,9171,903391,00.html.

Toben, Bradley J.B. and Kris Helge. "Sexual Misconduct of Clergypersons with Congregants or Parishioners – Civil and Criminal Liabilities and Responsibilities." Waco: Baylor University, 2009. http://www.baylor.edu/clergysexualmisconduct/index.php?id=63297.

Unitarian Universalist Association. *Restorative Justice for All: Unitarian Universalists Responding to Clergy Sexual Misconduct.* Boston: Unitarian Universalist Association, 2002. http://archive.uua.org/cde/csm/index.html.

Vickerman, Katherine A. and Gayla Margolin. "Rape Treatment Outcome Research: Empirical Findings and State of the Literature." *Clinical Psychology Review* 29 (2009): 431-448.

Wallace, Pat. "How Can She Still Love Him? Domestic Violence and the Stockholm Syndrome," *Community Practice* 80, no. 10 (2007): 32-34.

Waxman, Sharon, "Sioux Allege Abuse at Church Boarding Schools." *Washington Post,* June 2, 2003.

White, Gayle. "Sexual Misconduct: Keeping Vigil: How Various Faiths Protect the Innocent." *Atlanta Journal Constitu tion* (September 14, 2002): B1.Wisconsin. *Act 275.* 1985.

Weitz, Mark A. *Clergy Malpractice in America: Nally v. Grace Community Church of the Valley.* Lawrence, Kansas: University Press of Kansas, 2001.

Williams, Marleen S., Annette Jerome, Kirsten White, and Aaron Fisher, "Making Sense of Suffering: A Preliminary Study of Changes in Religious Women Adjusting to Severe Adversity," *Counseling and Values* 50 (2006): 84-98.

Recommended Reading

This section offers introductory reading on topics such as bodywork and dreamwork, which some of the laborers found helpful. It also provides resources on healing, the history of violence against women, clergy (professional) sexual assault, clergy malpractice, and spirituality.

Bodywork/Energy Work

Some of the laborers found body or energy work to be helpful in their healing. The following three books are introductions to such work.

Judith, Anodea. *Wheels of Life: A User's Guide to the Chakra System.* Woodbury: Llewellyn, 2003.

Smith, Linda, L. *Called into Healing: Reclaiming Our Judeo-Christian Legacy of Healing Touch.* Arvada: STM Press, 2000.

Wauters, Ambika. *The Book of Chakras: Discover the Hidden Forces within You.* New York: Quarto, 2002.

Dreamwork

Dreams were mentioned as a healing resource by some laborers because, at a time when they could not trust others and sometimes struggled with trusting themselves, they found the messages and the wisdom embedded in their dreams to be healing. Listed below are a few introductory books on dreams.

Guiley, Rosemary Ellen. *Dreamwork for the Soul: A Spiritual Guide to Dream Interpretation.* New York: Berkeley Books, 1998.

Jung, C.G. *Memories, Dreams, Reflections.* Recorded and edited by Aniela Jaffé, translated by Richard and Clara Winston. New York: Vintage Books, 1989.

Kaplan, Connie. *Dreams Are Letters from the Soul: Discover the Connections between Your Dreams and Your Spiritual Life.* New York: Harmony Books, 2002.

Kelsey, Morton T. *God, Dreams, and Revelation: A Christian Interpretation of Dreams.* Minneapolis: Augsburg, 1991.

Healing

The following books focus on various aspects of healing, such as forgiveness and relationships.

Carnes, Patrick J. *The Betrayal Bond: Breaking Free of Exploitive Relationships.* Deerfield Beach: Health Communications, 1997.

Hollis, Linda H. *Inner Healing for Broken Vessels.* Cleveland: Pilgrim Press, 2006.

Linn, Dennis, Sheila Fabricant Linn and Matthew Linn. *Don't Forgive Too Soon: Extending the Two Hands that Heal.* New York: Paulist Press, 1997.

Linn, Matthew, Sheila Fabricant Linn, and Dennis Linn. *Healing Spiritual Abuse and Religious Addiction.* New York: Paulist Press, 1994.

Markova, Dawna. *No Enemies Within: A Creative Process for Discovering What's Right About What's Wrong.* Berkeley: Conari, 1994.

Myss, Caroline. *Why People Don't Heal and How They Can.* New York: Random House, 1997.

Nouwen, Henri J.M. *The Wounded Healer: In Our Own Woundedness, We Can Become a Source of Life for Others.* New York: Image Books Doubleday, 1990.

Clergy (Professional) Sexual Assault

Some books on clergy sexual assault are listed in the Works Cited list. The following titles are in addition to those resources. *Lillie's Redemption* is the only novel on the list; it portrays the aftermath of clergy sexual assault and abuse as a small community begins to heal.

Byrne, Kathryn R. *Understanding the Abuse of Adults by Catholic Clergy and Religious.* Loganville: Morris Publishing, 2010.

Fortune, Marie M. and James N. Poling. *Sexual Abuse by Clergy: A Crisis for the Church.* Eugene: Wipf and Stock, 1994.

Friedman, Joel and Marcia Mobilia Boumil. *Betrayal of Trust: Sex and Power in Professional Relationships* Westport: Praeger, 1995.

Hopkins, Nancy Myer and Mark Laaser, Eds. *Restoring the Soul of a Church: Healing Congregations Wounded by Clergy Sexual Misconduct.* Collegeville: Alban Institute, 1995.

Horst, Elisabeth A. *Questions and Answers about Clergy Sexual Misconduct.* Collegeville: Liturgical Press, 2000.

Horst, Elisabeth A. *Recovering the Lost Self: Shame-Healing for Clergy Sexual Abuse.* Collegeville: Liturgical Press, 1998.

Meyer, Lydia Waring. *Lillie's Redemption.* Wyoming, MI: Prinicipa Media, 2011.

Mosgofian, Peter and George Ohlschlager. *Sexual Misconduct in Counseling and Ministry.* Dallas: Word, 1995.

Poling, James Newton. *The Abuse of Power: A Theological Problem.* Nashville: Abingdon Press, 1991.

Poling, Nancy Werking, ed. *Victim to Survivor: Women Recovering from Clergy Sexual Abuse.* Cleveland: United Church Press, 1999.

Shupe, Anson. *In the Name of All That's Holy: A Theory of Clergy Malfeasance.* Westport: Praeger, 1995.

Spirituality

These books are from a variety of spiritual traditions and are in addition to the resources listed in the Works Cited.

Adams, Carol Hamblet. *My Beautiful Broken Shell: Words of Hope to Refresh the Soul.* Eugene: Harvest House Publishers, 1998.

Chodron, Pema. *The Places that Scare You: A Guide to Fearlessness in Difficult Times.* Boston: Shambhala, 2001.

Chodron, Pema. *When Things Fall Apart: Heart Advice for Difficult Times.* Boston: Shambhala, 1997.

Fox, Matthew. *Creation Spirituality: Liberating Gifts for the Peoples of the Earth.* San Francisco: Harper, 1991.

Fox, Matthew. *Original Blessing.* New York: Jeremy P. Tarcher/Putman, 2000.

Ingerman, Sandra. *Soul Retrieval: Mending the Fragmented Self.* San Francisco: Harper, 1991.

McKenna, Megan. *Send My Roots Rain: A Spirituality of Justice and Mercy.* New York: Doubleday, 2003.

Moore, Thomas. *Care of the Soul: A Guide for Cultivating Depth and Sacredness in Everyday Life.* New York: HaperPerennial, 1992.

Ruiz, Don Miguel. *The Four Agreements.* San Rafael: Amber-Allen Publishing, 1997.

Ruiz, Don Miguel. *The Voice of Knowledge.* San Rafael: Amber-Allen Publishing, 2004.

Taylor, Barbara Brown. *Leaving Church: A Memoir of Faith.* San Francisco: Harper, 2006.

Thurman, Howard. *Jesus and the Disinherited.* Boston: Beacon Press, 1976.

Trauma

These books are resources on working through trauma.

Copeland, Mary Ellen and Maxine Harris. *Healing the Trauma of Abuse: A Woman's Workbook.* Oakland: New Harbinger Publications, 2000.

Cori, Jasmin L. *Healing from Trauma: A Survivor's Guide to Understanding Your Symptoms and Reclaiming Your Life.* New York: Marlowe and Company, 2008.

Levine, Peter A. *Healing Trauma: A Pioneering Program for Restoring the Wisdom of Your Body.* Boulder: Sounds True, 2008.

Levine, Peter A. *Walking the Tiger: Healing Trauma.* Berkeley: North Atlantic Books, 1997.

Rosenbloom, Dena, Mary Beth Williams with Barbara E. Watkins. *Life After Trauma: A Workbook for Healing.* New York: The Guilford Press, 2010.

Williams, Mary Beth and Soili Poijula. *The PTSD Workbook.* Oakland: New Harbinger Publications, 2002.

Journal Articles

Connor, Kathryn M., Jonathan R.T. Davidson and Li-Ching Lee. "Spirituality, Resilience, and Anger in Survivors of Violent Trauma: A Community Survey." *Journal of Traumatic Stress* 16 (2003): 487-494.

Disch, Estelle and Nancy Avery. "Sex in the Consulting Room, the Examining Room, and the Sacristy: Survivors of Sexual Abuse by Professionals." *American Journal of Orthopsychiatry,* 71 (2001): 204-217.

Doyle, Thomas P. "The Darkest of the Dark Side: The Catholic Hierarchy and Clergy Sexual Abuse." *Conscience,* Spring (2007): 34-36.

Doyle, Thomas P. "The Spiritual Trauma Experienced by Victims of Sexual Abuse by Catholic Clergy." *Pastoral Psychology,* 58 (2009): 239-260.

Evinger, James S. "Investigation and Disposition of Formal Ecclesiastical Cases of Pastoral Misconduct Involving Sexual Abuse: A Quantitative Study." *Journal of Religion and Abuse* 2 (2001): 5-30.

Flynn, Kathryn A. "In Their Own Voices: Women Who Were Sexually Abused by Members of the Clergy." *Journal of Child Sexual Abuse* 17 (2008): 216-237.

Murray-Swank, Nichole A. and Kenneth I. Pargament. "God, Where Are You?: Evaluating a Spiritually - Integrated Intervention for Sexual Abuse." *Mental Health, Religion and Culture* 8 (2005): 191-203.

Neustein, Amy and Michael Lesher. "A Single-Case Study of Rabbinic Sexual Abuse in the Orthodox Jewish Community." *Journal of Child Sexual Abuse* 17 (2008): 270-89.

Rose, Susan D. "Telling Lives: Trauma-Recovery and Christian-Conversion Narratives." *Journal of Religion and Abuse* 4 (2002): 33-67.

van Wormer, Katherine and Lois Berns. "The Impact of Priest Sexual Abuse: Female Survivors' Narratives." *Affilia: Journal of Women and Social Work* 19 (2004): 53-67.